HOW TO BE A THOUSANDAIRE

Catherine Adamson

woven word

How to be a Thousandaire
Copyright © Catherine Adamson 2019
ISBN 978-1-913170-06-6

All rights reserved. No part of this publication may be reproduced or distributed in any form or by any means, or stored in a database or electronic retrieval system without the prior written permission of Fisher King Publishing Ltd. Thank you for respecting the author of this work.

Published by:
Woven Word
An Imprint of Fisher King Publishing Ltd
The Studio
Arthington Lane
Pool in Wharfedale
LS21 1JZ
England
www.fisherkingpublishing.co.uk

Illustrations and cover design by Annina Diston
using resources from Freepik.com

Thousandaire®
Trade Mark Registered in Great Britain and Northern Ireland

Dedicated to:

My dad who is loved and missed every day and who would have been so proud of me.

My Heartfelt Thanks to:

Nikki Coverdale for her loyal support throughout my journey and for being an incredible friend and human being, Gayle Johnson for showing me how to breathe life into my writing, the whole Kaleidoscope team without whom I wouldn't have a business, and everyone I have ever worked with whose energy and enthusiasm have powered me forward.

My Love to:

My fabulous husband Bill for his love and support and for always believing in me, and my friend Sarah Izzard for her words of inspiration and encouragement.

'A journey of a thousand miles
begins with a single step'
Lao-Tze

Contents

Foreword — i

Hello and welcome! — 1

1 WHAT'S IMPORTANT TO YOU? — 7

2 WHERE ARE YOU NOW?
    Are you being your best you? — 29

3 WHERE ARE YOU NOW?
    Is your business working for you? — 47

4 WHERE DO YOU WANT TO BE? — 67

5 GETTING READY: Mindset & Behaviours — 87

6 GETTING READY: The Practicalities — 113

7 MAKING IT HAPPEN — 141

8 KEEPING IT GOING — 169

CONCLUSION — 193

Appendices — 201

Foreword

What makes an inspiring leader? This is a question I've spent my career asking and answering. It's one of the most important questions of our time. Leadership affects us all - how we live, how we work, how we do business. It shapes the world we live in.

In this book, Catherine tackles many questions close to my heart, with the microbusiness world as her focus. It's a much-needed addition to the conversations around leadership and doing successful, inspiring business.

Often when people think about leadership they picture CEOs of large, global organisations. But that's not where leadership starts. It starts with ourselves. And in 'How To Be A Thousandaire' Catherine sets out the qualities and behaviours needed to become an effective personal and organisational leader.

This book doesn't hold back. Catherine walks the talk of leadership, setting out her mistakes, learning and triumphs in equal measure. We need to experience life lessons for ourselves, but it makes sense to learn from those who have gone before us. And what you have here is a pocket guide to getting the foundations of business right so you set the stage for sustainable growth.

In my own book, 'Inspiring Women Leaders' I share the stories of over 100 leaders who are brave, vulnerable and honest in their accounts of where they got it right, where they got it wrong, and what they had to overcome to become the leaders they are today. Some attributes are common to them all. Their moral integrity, for example - their ability to stay true to themselves and their values, no matter what. And their resilience – they get back up again and again despite the inevitable setbacks. That's what you'll see as Catherine shares her own experiences.

These same qualities are needed of any aspiring business owner, whatever scale you're working at, wherever you are in your business journey. This book offers you warts and all insight into what it takes to be a microbusiness leader and how to keep going when the curveballs hit, whether you're just starting out or have been in business for a while and are looking for growth.

The Thousandaire model isn't just a theory. It works. Catherine's had her fair share of personal loss, and when the life crises hit her business survived and thrived. All because she had done the groundwork she shares here. Being a Thousandaire is an achievable ambition for every microbusiness owner.

This is no 'get rich quick' scheme – if something sounds too good to be true, it probably is. There's work involved – being an inspiring leader is a full time responsibility! It's all about identifying your values, priorities and strengths. And from there it's about the practical business savvy to get things moving and growing. You'll find all of that in these pages.

I fervently believe that the world needs more of us to step up as inspiring leaders. This is a good place to start. If you're a microbusiness owner, or someone thinking about how to start up a business the right way for growth and success, this is the book for you. I hope you enjoy it as much as I did.

Leigh Bowman-Perks
CEO of Inspiring Leadership International and
Author of Inspiring Women Leaders

Hello and welcome!

I'm so pleased you have made the decision to explore how to create and grow a microbusiness. And not just any business, but one that balances time, money and energy in a way that allows you to fulfil your dreams and aspirations.

The Thousandaire model is about finding trusted associates who can replicate what you do and allow you to increase your client base beyond your personal capacity, resulting in you reaching your lifestyle nirvana of enough money, enough time and enough energy – now doesn't that sounds like a good place to be?

Everything in this book will help you achieve just that. To get there you'll need clear values, an ongoing passion for your business, and a client and team-centric approach to everything you do.

I'll be encouraging you to consider what success looks like for you as a microbusiness owner. It's not about judging your success against the success of other people, it's not about achieving riches beyond your wildest dreams, and it's not about growing a business which uses people as a disposable resource. It is about finding your own Thousandaire Sweet Spot so you can do business well and live well.

I know for many of us in business life feels like one, hard juggle of long days, weekend working and not being paid unless you're at the grindstone.

I also know that it's possible to build a business that gives you space to do more of the things you love and want to do, and to live life with more ease. I know because I've done it. That's not because I'm some master strategist with insider secrets. It's because I needed to.

In 2014 we lost two children after our adoption broke down, and the trauma of all that almost broke me. It dominated my life for nearly four years. Luckily, I'd already laid the foundations for resilience in my business – I'm a natural planner and I wanted to ensure my business would survive the adoption transition. Little did I know how much more complex and difficult my life would become as the situation unfolded. I can honestly say that if I hadn't created a team around my business, it wouldn't be here now. And the stress of trying to work, work, work through all of that would have pushed me under too.

Now I'm no longer in the raw hurt of that loss, my thriving Thousandaire business has enabled me to focus my life on things I value – like being outside, volunteering and developing my leadership skills so I can support my team better. I was able to raise £10,000 for charity in 2018 – a feat that would not have been possible if I was still constantly at the coal face of my business.

So, for me, being a Thousandaire isn't just a practical, accessible business model. It's a way of working out what's important to you in life and creating a business that gives you the space to do those important things. It's good for your community and your loved ones as well as being good for you!

Whether you're already in business and curious about how to make it work better for you, or whether you're just starting out, creating a microbusiness that feeds into your Thousandaire Sweet Spot is key to a happy, balanced life.

That is true for all of us, and within reach for all of us. It's all about breaking it down, seeking support and taking action.

Through this book, my Facebook page (Catherine Adamson - Author Mentor Speaker) and my website (www.catherineadamson.co.uk) I want us to forge connections while we learn how to strengthen and grow our businesses so they can survive any curveballs life throws our way. Feel free to take a look and to become part of our online community. It's all totally free and you will receive a very warm welcome.

Are you ready for growth?

It's a tricky time for any microbusiness owner when you have been in business for a couple of years, you have a steady flow of work, and you are kept busy not only juggling your client work but also trying to manage the day to day running of your business. You're not only on the front line delivering your service or making your product, you're also Marketing Director, Sales Director, Financial Controller, Head of IT, Customer Service Manager… you get the point here, yes?

Things can sometimes come unstuck when you reach workload capacity – after all you only have one pair of hands. When you're running a microbusiness the phrase 'time equals money' is truer than it will have ever been before for you. I clearly remember waking up in the middle of the night panicking because my workload was becoming unmanageable and, as a result, I'd forgotten to do something important. I then spent the next two hours at my laptop doing the work – that's not what I had in mind when I started my business!

Unfortunately, there's nothing we can do to increase the amount of time available to us. We just need to work smarter rather than harder. If you want to make more time you need to create more capacity, and that means growing your team to more than just you.

Maybe you're in a business and life rut? It's so easy when you work alone, and many of us are home workers, to find yourself running around in a great big business hamster wheel. Every day can start to feel the same. The work you are doing may feel less than inspiring because you're no longer challenged by it. You can so easily start to fall out of love with the business that you were once so passionate about. It's probably true for all of us at some point in our journey of self-employment but it can start to feel overwhelmingly negative and impossible to climb out of. It's at this stage that you need to make some positive changes in your business to bring it, and you, back to life.

So, how do you do that?

You need to step away. You, as an individual, must grow from being an employee in your own business, and become the business owner. You need to change how you feel about yourself and your role in your own business. Only then can you start planning and creating a business that is resilient and keeps going even when you're not there.

As I mentioned earlier, this book is for values and relationship driven businesses. It is for those of you who, like me, want to remain engaged and in love with your business. The people I work with really matter to me - without them I wouldn't still have a business. I respect every one of my team members as well as our clients who keep my business going. It's not about me outsourcing work to make my life easier and richer at the expense of anyone else, it's about making my business work for all of us. Yes, I am earning more money now, but I am also really proud of the fact that I can give work to other people, and that the relationships we have with our clients are our highest priority – we don't dilute our service to make more money, we enhance our service to ensure quality and client satisfaction.

Having said all of that, it takes courage to trust someone else with your business. It takes courage to think of the costs involved in delegating work as an investment. It takes courage to take that first step into the unknown and risk everything to evolve and grow your business. When you work alone and are responsible for making all the decisions, small and large, taking the leap can feel scary, and it is certainly far easier to do nothing. But doing nothing will result in nothing changing, and I really hope that you want to change.

Your business, your way

This book is my story, my journey: it's not a one size fits all blueprint to success. We all run different businesses and some of you may benefit from everything in here, some of you may want to pick and choose whatever you think will work for you. I can say, hand on heart, that everything in the book worked for me in my business. It is all tried and tested by yours truly, and even if some chapters are less relevant for you, I encourage you to read through them anyway. You just never know where you might find that hidden gem.

It's an honest insider look at my successes and my failures, with tips, strategies, and thought processes that all helped me to achieve the business growth, lifestyle balance and freedom you are aiming for.

I talk about vision and goal setting, the huge importance of values in your business, the ups and downs of recruitment and outsourcing, how to successfully work from home, the strength that you can find within yourself and absolutely loads more.

I will be guiding you through the process of your business growth in easy to follow step by step stages. We start with setting your vision and understanding where you are now, then we'll look at where you want to be in your business, onto developing your personal and business skills and habits, right through to keeping things going once you achieve your goals. Each topic has been split down into three sections. Firstly, the bare bones information that you will need to progress, secondly, examples from my business with top tips and strategies to help keep you on the straight and narrow, and lastly a key points section to give you a quick reference if you need reminding at any time.

You will see me refer to a Thousandaire journal as you progress through the book, look for the journal icon in the margin. There are several exercises that you will need to revisit and reflect on as you move forward and it's a good idea to keep them all in one place so get yourself a nice new pad and keep it with you as you read on.

I sincerely hope that what I share makes as much difference to you and your business as it did for me and mine.

And remember, this is your journey, and a journey of a thousand miles begins with a single step… Bon voyage!

Chapter One
WHAT'S IMPORTANT TO YOU?
Setting your vision and values

> 'Never tell me the sky's the limit when
> there are footprints on the moon'
> Unknown

All too often we are surrounded by other people's definitions of what success looks like. We're told what success 'should' look like to all of us, and usually wealth, status, and celebrity seem to feature at the top of the list.

As microbusiness owners we're all on our own journey. I know from experience how easy it is to veer off our own path to accommodate this notion of success that society pushes upon us. It can be tricky to stay true to ourselves when there's so much external pressure to conform. So, it's important for us to create a place to stand: a clear sense of why we're in business and what we want our life to look like. To write our own rulebook.

This chapter will give you the tools to do just that. I will be sharing and guiding you through a few simple ways to create your business and personal vision and helping you to think about what values you hold most dear.

By the end of this chapter, you'll have a better understanding of:

- what success looks like to you
- what's important to you as an individual, a family member, a friend, and as a business owner
- what you value
- what you want

- your Thousandaire Sweet Spot

Shortly after setting up in business I attended a local networking event. I was nervous as networking was a new thing to me, and excited as I was keen to get word out about my business and how fabulous it was. I met many interesting people at this event, but only one still stands out in my mind.

I was approached by a gentleman in a very smart suit who looked like he really meant business. After explaining that I had just become self-employed, he guffawed (honestly, laughter is too modest a word for what he did) and proceeded to tell me what a nightmare the rest of my life would be – 24/7 working hours, no holidays, no weekends, no life basically. He was also self-employed, and had been for many years, and it was obvious to me that this non-stop working philosophy was what had happened to him and he appeared to be proud of it.

I made my mind up right then and there that things were going to be different for me. What was the point of being self-employed if I was going to enslave myself? Surely there had to be benefits to working for myself?

Hmmm. I wonder what those benefits could be? Perhaps setting your own work patterns depending on what works best for you? Or being totally in control of your own destiny? Hey, and what about being able to take holidays without having to get permission from your boss – that's a good one, don't you think?

That gentleman did me a favour. Right from the start he showed me that we have a choice about how we do business. There is no one size fits all solution.

So, the million-dollar question is: What do you want out of your business? What makes you tick?

Choose your lifestyle

I became self-employed because I wanted more control, not less, and from the outset I organised my business to give me the work-life balance I wanted. I believe being committed to your work also involves being committed to your own well-being (or committed is what you will be – to an institution!).

In my experience most microbusiness owners set up because they are passionate about what they do, whatever that is. Personally, I don't think it would be possible to run a microbusiness that you didn't feel passion for – how could you spend your days and hours in a business of your own that you didn't find rewarding? If you're passionate about what you do, you want to feel pride in the business that is growing around you. You want to be proud of yourself, proud of what you do, and proud of how you do it.

However, we all need more than passion to make a successful business. As your dream becomes reality you need to ensure all the compulsory 'boring' aspects of self-employment happen too. This requires a big change in attitude – this isn't a hobby, however much you love doing it.

So, what do you need to keep going when you feel like you are sinking under the day to day essential tasks? 'Sinking' is exactly how I used to feel when everything in my business was done by me. I will be delving deeper into this feeling and giving you some advice on how to avoid it by successfully building a team around you later in the book. But for now – what you need to hold onto is a clear vision of your own.

Whatever your passion, whatever your motivation, don't listen to what other people think. It's inevitable that you will come across people who seem to enjoy telling you how hard things are going to be, and who seem to thrive on encouraging others to struggle. Ignore them. Listen to what you feel and develop a vision to match.

If you want to work flexible hours to suit your body clock, then plan for that to happen. If you want to have six months' holiday a year then plan for that too. Don't discount anything as being too ambitious if it's what you truly want. It might not happen all at once but if you don't plan for it then it will probably never happen at all. Be positive and you will reap the rewards.

The Thousandaire Sweet Spot

We live in a world where the very word 'success' has been hijacked by those who think they are hugely successful and compare themselves to others they deem less successful or even unsuccessful. Many books about growing a business have at their very essence the promise of you becoming rich beyond your wildest dreams and therefore achieving success.

But what is enough for you? What does success look like for you? Consider what you want your life to look like in terms of the amount of time you have available for things other than work, your energy levels, how much money you need to live a balanced and happy life, and your overall physical, mental and emotional well-being.

Success shouldn't just be gauged on how much money we can accumulate. There's our whole work life balance to consider as well.

Not everyone with lots of money is happy. I'm sure we've all read about people who have so much money they really don't know what to do with it: perhaps they've won the lottery, perhaps they have worked hard to achieve their wealth — but they're not always happy.

Forever grasping for more of everything is the route to unhappiness and discontent for us all. Being contented is a beautiful place to be. I remember on the day my Dad passed away, we were talking about reincarnation, and I asked him what, if he could be reincarnated, he would like to come back as. His reply to me has always stayed with me. He said: 'I don't want anything different or anything more than what I've got now'.

This totally blew me away! Even in his last moments he wasn't grasping for something bigger or better – he was content, he was happy. I can only hope that I feel the same when my time comes.

So, take time to think about what is enough for you. Enough money, enough time, enough energy, enough of the good stuff in life that feeds our souls as well as our wallets. Here are a few questions to help you along – take out your Thousandaire journal and write your answers down:

1. How much money is enough money? Consider your day to day living, your leisure and hobbies, holidays and short breaks, charitable giving, savings, and anything else that you want as part of your life.

2. How much time do you need to live the life you want to live? Time to work on the future of your business, time to be with loved ones, time on hobbies, time being part of your community. Time is the one thing we can't get more of. But you can prioritise the time you have. Consider how much of your time you want to spend working, playing or simply relaxing and watching the world go by.

3. How do you want to feel? How much energy do you want to have? As a microbusiness owner, you are your biggest asset and it's important to look after yourself. How much rest and sleep do you need for you to be at your best? Are you nourishing your body with healthy food and regular meal times? Are you getting enough down time and

doing the things that feed your soul?

Keep your answers safe as you'll be referring to this again later in the book.

Once you have your answers to these questions you will reach what I call 'The Thousandaire Sweet Spot'. Your future success will now be about what you want to achieve and not what others think you should be achieving. It's about rating yourself against yourself, and not comparing yourself to others or even considering what others think success is. It's a very personal concept and important to complete (so if you've skipped answering the questions, do it now before reading any further!).

Building your vision

Okay, so you've thought about your sweet spot. That's a great starting point. Now you need to figure out what your motivation is. The best and most effective way to do this is to 'build your vision'.

Without a vision for your business (and of course your life) how will you know when it all starts to come true? Your vision can include anything that's important to you, anything around your business growth and aspirations, personal challenges, lifestyle aspirations, family and friends, anything that you want to achieve, improve or deliver. The world is your oyster when it comes to your vision.

When I first set up in business, back in 2008, I had a clear vision of a few things I really wanted to have. Top of that list was a cleaner, oh how I wanted a cleaner! I also wanted a huge squidgy sofa – I lived in a small terrace house at the time and a huge sofa was not only out of my price bracket, it was also totally impractical. There would literally be no more room in the lounge. But it was still part of my vision and guess what? I now have a huge squidgy sofa.

A more recent vision exercise included my dream to raise £10,000 for charity by walking and wild camping The Cleveland Way. I included pictures of the route and words describing how I would feel once I'd achieved my dream. I completed my challenge in August 2018 and being able to visualise how I would feel and what it would look like made it far easier to make it come true.

Here's an exercise to help you develop your vision

Close your eyes, pick a date and a time in the future, and focus on the details of what is going on for you, your nearest and dearest, and your business. Make sure you think in the present tense, for example, 'I am being presented with an award', rather than 'I want to win an award'.

Ask yourself: Where will I be? What will I be doing? What am I wearing? Who am I with? What is happening in my business? Who is working in my business? What can I see? What can I hear? The list goes on... The more detail the better, and the more you feel it the better.

Be loud and proud with your vision, create the life you want for yourself, and remember there are no barriers, no right and wrong, just a blank page that you can fill. It's your vision and you can make it whatever you want it to be.

Once you have done this take a step back and think about how you will feel when you have achieved your vision. Really think about how you were feeling at that precise moment in time that you picked earlier. I remember when I first did this exercise, I was so excited about what the future had in store for me. I felt incredible, I felt empowered and I felt ready to rule the world! I just couldn't wait to get started!

Then take another step back and consider the opposite. How will you feel if you don't achieve your vision? My feelings were overwhelmingly negative. I felt disappointed in myself and I felt physically unsettled and out of sorts.

These feelings, both positive and negative, are your motivation to get started and build your business to where you want it to be. Listen to them: use them to fuel your progress and check back with yourself from time to time. Your feelings are like your compass - they're there to direct you and they're worth listening to – I promise!

Once you've completed this exercise, I invite you to set up a play date with yourself.

Does that sound a bit strange? Bear with me!

Get yourself prepared with some paper, glue, glitter pens, magazines and anything else that floats your creative boat. You're going to create your vision board.

Your vision board

A vision board is simply a visual representation of where you want to be. You can use whatever you like to create it. Cut our images, words, doodle, add photos, add pictures of role models or mentors, whatever works for you.

Be as playful as possible – enjoy the process and dream. Don't tie yourself down by practicalities at this stage (if I'd let the practicality of having a small terraced house stop me dreaming, I wouldn't have my squidgy sofa today!). This is about feeling free to be who you want to be, living the life you want to live, running the business you want to live.

Then put it somewhere near to your desk so you can look at it every day. On days when everything just feels too tough, you can spend a few moments looking at your vision board and reminding yourself why it's all worth it.

I promise you, it won't be too long before you can start ticking things off your vision board as you'll have achieved them. Yay!!!

Don't ever forget though, this is your vision. Flexibility is key here. If you want to change your vision you can at any time – it's yours! Nobody else can ever tell you what it should be and nobody else will ever know if you have updated it to suit any changes in your life or your circumstances. So, feel free to stick and then unstick if that's what you want to do. Own it!

So, you now have a clear vision of where you are going. You should be proud of yourself at this point as most microbusiness owners don't have what you now have. They really don't! You would be amazed how many business owners just go with the flow and wait to see what happens. This is an easy option, and some may find it works for them. But having a clear vision really provides you with the focus and clarity for conscious decision-making, planning and ultimately achieving your dreams.

Figuring out what makes you tick

Another important, and often ignored, aspect of running a microbusiness is to fully understand what makes you tick. What do you stand for? What are your values? Like your vision, your values will provide you with a clear direction. They are a compass to follow during the good and the not so good times.

When I first set up in business, I thought I understood what my values were. But I hadn't spent any time at all thinking them through and aligning them with what I was doing, I didn't understand how they impacted and reflected on my business, my team members, my clients, and all other people who encountered me and my business.

This was a mistake.

I discovered how important it was for me to be clear on my values when I was challenged by a client about the very essence of my business model. I was unprepared for how this would make me feel, I was shaken to the core, and I was forced to reflect on and decide upon my core values. I could no longer pretend I knew what they were, I had to know what they were deep down inside. I then had to literally fight to keep my values at the centre of everything I did: constantly referring to them to ensure that what I was doing and saying reflected what I believed was important to not only my business, but to me personally. It was an exhausting experience and one which, without clear business values, may have left me regretting my decisions.

I can now reflect on my experience and although I clearly made the right decisions, I will also learn from the mistakes I made – not communicating clearly enough and making assumptions that others knew what I wanted. After all, one of my core values is courage so learning from mistakes is a key part of this.

Understanding your values not only enhances what you can offer, but it also makes decision making in your business so much easier. Values based decision making keeps things honest. Whatever the outcome of your decision you will sleep at night knowing that your intentions were always good.

So, what are values?

Values are the basis for how you live your life. They run throughout your personal and work life. They influence the decisions you make, your priorities in life, and they signpost your way forward. Your values are what you always stand for. They are the 'why' that supports all your actions.

We all know how it feels when we behave in a way that doesn't fit with our values. It can leave us feeling dissatisfied and out of sorts, unhappy. For example, if you value family, but you are working 7 days a week, do you think you will be happy? If you value calm, but leave all your work to the last minute, do you think you will be calm? Or do you think you will be stressed and anxious?

I always think of a sunflower when I think of my values. A sunflower will move throughout the day to face the sun, is flexible enough to bend with the wind, and yet remains firmly rooted. Whatever happens to it, whatever is going on around it, it is always a sunflower.

The roots are our values that ground us and support our behaviours; the stem represents our behaviours that are our values in action; the flower is the resulting 'Authentic You!'

In business, like in life, things will happen around you. Sometimes you will be put off your stride, and you may be influenced and tempted to take the easy way out (often contrary to your values). When this happens, be like a sunflower. Move toward what nourishes you and be flexible with what you expect from other people yet remain firmly rooted in your values. They are your strength.

The truth is clear: acting according to our values results in us feeling happy and content. Even if things go wrong, we always know that our decisions have come from a good place.

Deciding upon which key values represent you is not an easy thing to do. To help you I have listed below a few common values that I invite you to reflect upon and consider before reading any further:

Humour	Zest	Integrity
Love	Courage	Respect
Honesty	Spirituality	Innovation
Gratitude	Fun	Excellence
Fairness	Teamwork	Customer focus
Kindness	Judgement	Trust
Hope	Love of learning	Diversity
Perseverance	Prudence	Accountability
Curiosity	Perspective	Community
Forgiveness	Creativity	Collaboration
Calmness	Humility	Commitment
Leadership	Wisdom	Happiness

I thought it might be useful for me to share my personal values with you at this stage. I regularly reflect on these values when I'm having a bad day, if I need to deal with a situation that makes me feel uncomfortable, or if I have a big decision to make. They are so important to my day to day functioning that quite frankly I don't know what I would do without them. They are no longer just words. They are my route through life.

Happiness

This may sound like an obvious choice, but happiness can be an elusive concept. I believe that if I want to be happy, I need to be happy on purpose. It's an active decision that I focus on daily. When I wake up,

I don't just wait to see what kind of day I'll have. I make an active decision to have a happy day.

Calmness

I consider calmness to be a superpower and I encourage and nurture a culture of calmness throughout my business. If I am stressed or anxious, I am not the best version of me. If I am calm, I feel in control, able to make good decisions, and able to deal with tricky situations. Being calm keeps my mind clear and gives me peace.

Kindness

I believe in being kind to myself when I make a mistake (as we all do), or if I just need a little more nurturing from time to time. I believe in being kind to others – you just don't know what kind of day they're having. Thinking kind thoughts, rather than thinking the worst, feeds my soul.

Courage

> "You can choose courage, or you can choose comfort, but you cannot choose both."
> Brene Brown

For me courage is doing the things that I find hard. Having those difficult conversations, facing a personal or business challenge, being out of my comfort zone but doing it anyway. For me, being out of my comfort zone means I am stretching myself and moving forward.

Honesty

This is so important to me. I believe that honesty should run throughout everything I do and say. I believe in having honest conversations where agendas are clearly identified. I believe in being honest in my actions and showing an authenticity in everything I do.

Getting clear on your values will give you a rock-solid foundation for your business – both at the start and as it grows. So, let's get practical and explore how you can do this.

Here's an exercise to help you to reflect on and identify your values:

Firstly, give yourself some time and find a quiet space where you're not going to be disturbed.

You're going to be doing a lot of thinking about this, so I encourage you to make some notes in your Thousandaire journal as you go to keep track of your thoughts and emotions. Ask yourself the following questions:

- What makes me feel happy and fulfilled?
- When was I at my best and why?
- What accomplishments am I most proud of?
- What have I done that I regret or that was unsuccessful?
- How did this make me feel?
- Who inspires me and why?
- Which of their traits do I admire and want to develop in myself?
- What traits in other people do I least admire?
- How would I describe myself in 10 words or less?

Then…fill in the blanks:

- I believe in…
- I care about…
- I value…

Then… ask yourself, what is my deal breaker? What one value matters the most to you? Which one could you not live without?

My deal breaker is kindness. I can't bear to see anyone being unkind in either words or actions. Witnessing unkindness will immediately affect the relationship I have with someone. There's a saying that I love, 'Kindness is free, sprinkle that stuff everywhere', and that's what I always try to do.

Once you have completed this it would be a useful exercise to ask other people what they would say about you. This can be an uncomfortable thing to do (especially if you want them to be honest) but it will give you a better idea on how you are perceived by others, and an indication of whether your behaviours reflect your values. We will be talking about this further in the next chapter. For now, just keep it simple and give yourself the challenge of asking three people to name three values or attributes they associate with you. Write their responses in your Thousandaire journal.

My critical moment

A critical moment in my understanding of the power of values came when I watched a Ted Talk by Simon Sinek entitled 'How great leaders inspire action'. It helped me to better understand the power of understanding my own motivation and the values that influence and reinforce my actions.

Sinek describes how people don't buy what you do, they buy why you do it. Instead of running your business based upon 'what' you do and 'how' you do it, you need to run your business based on 'why' you do it – your passion, your beliefs, your purpose. He goes on to explain that our goal shouldn't be to do business with people who need what we do, our goal should be to do business with people who believe what we believe.

It's about how we make people feel. If you think about it for a moment, I am sure there are lots of people out there who do what you do, who offer the same service, or produce the same product. Why will someone buy from you instead of your competitor? Why do they choose you? It's because they believe what you believe, your values are aligned, they have bought your 'why'.

Knowing your values is knowing your 'why'. But knowing them and doing them are different. It's important to consider how other people experience your values. How are your values put into action? We will be looking at how our behaviours need to reflect our values in much more detail in the next chapter, but for now I thought you might find it useful for me to share what my value of 'calmness' means to me:

- ***To encourage and nurture a culture of calmness.*** I believe that good planning, effective communication and engaged team members enable a busy yet peaceful work environment in which we can all thrive.

- ***To approach problem solving in an open, honest and***

transparent way. I believe in a safe, no blame, solution focussed culture.

- ***To give our clients 'the phew factor'.*** To ensure that our clients are calm in the knowledge that their business is in safe and capable hands.

Hopefully you will now have a clear vision of where you are heading, you will have figured out what your Thousandaire Sweet Spot is, and you will be clear on what you value most in your life and in business. That is a great place to be! You have clarity on where you want to be.

The next chapter will focus on understanding where you are right now. Do your behaviours align with your values? Do you have the skills and processes in place that you need to achieve your vision? How are you spending your time and is it productive? You'll move on from thinking about the future to thinking about the present and taking steps to turn your future into your reality.

Key Points

- Know your vision – without a clear goal in mind how will you know how to get there or when you reach it?

- Be flexible – life happens to us all. Take account of changes in your circumstances and re-think your vision from time to time to make sure it is still what you want.

- Understand your own motivation – is it reputation, money, time, holidays, flexibility? What is your Thousandaire Sweet Spot?

- Be yourself – this isn't about comparing yourself to others, it's about creating your own unique foundation for business.

- Know your values – get clear on what is most important to you. This is your internal guidance system. Be a sunflower!

Chapter Two
WHERE ARE YOU NOW?
Are you being your best you?

> 'No one is you and that is your power.'
> Dave Grohl

On your blocks...

You now have a clear vision, and a deep-rooted understanding of your values. That's great! But before you start making plans and taking steps to realise your vision, I encourage you to sit back, take a long deep breath and reflect on where you are right now.

I love enthusiasm and I love being around enthusiastic people, but without clarity over your starting point how will you know how to get where you want to go?

Enthusiasm can overwhelm the practicalities of growing a business. Be enthusiastic but be realistic too. Knowing where you are right now will mean you can take decisive and measured actions towards your future.

If you were an elite athlete would you wander up to the start of a race and just start running? Or would you place your feet firmly on the blocks and wait for the starting pistol to be fired?

This chapter is about you finding your internal starting blocks, so when the pistol is fired you can really start to run. It's about performing a self-audit of your current 'inner world' reality and beginning to understand the practicalities of what you may need to take your first steps forward.

So, what do I mean by 'inner world'? This chapter isn't about the nuts and bolts of your business. It's about you as an integral part of your business: your mindset, your behaviours and your personal strengths and weaknesses. So, this is your opportunity to focus just on you.

Nobody else matters right now, just you. How lovely is that?

By the end of the chapter, you'll have clarity on your current:

- behaviours – do they reflect your values?
- skills – what are your personal strengths and weaknesses?
- work habits – do you treat yourself kindly or are you the boss from hell?
- support network – who keeps you grounded when the world around you is in chaos?

What you take from this chapter will be different for each of you. If you are a start-up this may be a simple exercise. But if you have been running a business for a few years you will probably have developed a few habits, both good and bad, and established behaviours that may or may not support your values, and you may need to spend more time reflecting on what's going on right now for you.

Whatever stage you're at: new business, first year or more established, it's a good idea to come back to this from time to time. Remember, each day in business is a new opportunity to firmly ground yourself. It can be easy to be busy doing nothing - believe me I used to be an expert in this! So, I find it useful to reflect on all of this from time to time to make sure I have my feet firmly on my starting blocks and that each day moves me forward.

Are you walking the walk?

In the previous chapter you spent time reflecting on questions that will hopefully have helped you to understand what you stand for, what your values are.

It's a wonderful thing to understand your values. On paper, they will enhance your decision-making process; they will help you to attract clients and customers who align with your values, people who buy your 'why'. Finding team members who value the same things as you will also become easier. In fact, everything, both in business and more broadly becomes easier - isn't that fabulous!

But paper isn't reality. The truth is, it's simple to write down a list of what we value, but it's far harder to put it into practice.

Being authentic is key to building and growing a business. At least it is if you are running a microbusiness. You are your business, and if your authenticity doesn't shine through then your business will suffer.

I know from experience how easy it can be to make a decision because I felt something was expected of me, and I thought I 'should', instead of focusing on my values and how I really felt about the situation. I clearly remember my 'gut feeling' telling me one thing but doing another. Trust me when I say that's not a great place to be. I lost sleep, I worried about it, and eventually I had the difficult job of reversing my decision. It was a challenging time for me, trusting my values, but putting them aside to please someone else. Ultimately, I got it sorted but a clear values-based decision from the start would have prevented all the confusion and upset that I caused myself.

So, are you authentic? Do you walk the walk as well as talk the talk?

How are your values experienced by others in what you say and what you do? Do your behaviours prove to you and to others that your values are authentic?

The following exercise will help you think about whether your actions and words align with your values. Remember though, we are talking about your current reality in this chapter. Be honest and realistic with yourself, but don't beat yourself up if things are a little out of line. We all get things wrong sometimes, and habits are hard to change. This is a learning curve, and consciously reflecting on your behaviours, acknowledging them and accepting them, and finally modifying them is all part of your growth.

Ask yourself the following questions and make a note of your answers in your Thousandaire journal:

Are my actions...

Fill the gap with your value i.e. honest, courageous, kind

How do I show this?

How do I prove to myself and others that I value this?

Are my words...

Fill the gap with your value i.e. honesty, courageous, kind

How do I show this?

How do I prove to myself and others that I value this?

To help you, here are a few examples from my own value – **Courage**

Are my actions courageous?

How do I show this?

1. I empower my team members and don't micro manage – good going for a control freak like me!
2. I am accountable for my mistakes – owning up and providing solutions instead of hiding mistakes and worrying about them.
3. I actively encourage myself to stretch outside my comfort zone.

Are my words courageous?
How do I show this?

1. I tackle tricky conversations head on – I say what I need to say. I'm kind and compassionate but I don't avoid the conversation because it's hard.
2. I will stand up for and support people if I see an injustice.
3. I'm honest when asked for an opinion. I'm kind but honest.

Are you a good boss?

Running your own business is amazing, isn't it? You can choose your working hours, take as many holidays as you want to, and even work in your pyjamas. Right? Well to a point you're right, of course - it's your business and it's your choice. You can in fact do whatever you want and call it work, and I've done plenty of that in my time! But the reality is at some point you will need to crack on with doing something constructive or you won't be in business for long.

It can take a while to settle into being self-employed and to finally release yourself from the employee mindset. I remember how I felt when I first became a microbusiness owner. I think it took me about six months to stop thinking like a Personal Assistant, and to start thinking like a professional service provider. I was no longer an employed PA. I was now a business owner who provided a professional PA service to my clients. The boundaries were different, the relationships were different, the expectations were different.

I could now pick and choose who my clients were; I was responsible for providing my clients with a contract, rather than my employer dictating what my terms were; and I was able to manage my time according to my priorities and not those of anyone else.

It was a wonderful feeling when I realised how much more control, freedom and flexibility I had. But along with all these wonderful positive outcomes came the realisation that I had to be my own boss. Running a business, especially if you work from home, requires structure and discipline.

I know that not all microbusiness owners work from home, but most of us do. I'm in the 'why spend money on office space when you can set up a home office for free?' camp. Though I know other successful microbusiness owners who wouldn't be without their separate workspace, often in a co-working area. They value the camaraderie you get from other business owners, and the self-imposed discipline you get when you are not being distracted by all those never-ending tasks that your home will generate, for example, ironing, walking the dog, and quite frankly, watching daytime television (I defy anyone to say they have never done this). You will know what suits you best.

Being your own boss means you must be exactly that, a boss. If you were an employee, I can guarantee that your boss wouldn't appreciate you spending hours watching television, sitting in your pyjamas, or turning up whenever you fancy for however long you fancy.

Working from home requires a special kind of discipline, and with more than a few years of self-employment behind me I've learned a lot about how to enjoy all the benefits of home working without giving in to the lure of the sofa, or an extra few hours in bed!

It's all about setting a good example for yourself and getting into habits that nurture rather than sabotage your business. Because that is what you will be doing if you don't develop a structure and balance to your work day.

So, this is your opportunity to self-review your performance as your own boss. Does that make sense? Basically, are you a good boss?

I invite you to take your Thousandaire journal and spend five minutes writing down your thoughts about 'you the boss'. Here are some prompts to get you thinking:

- Do I treat my work as a business or a hobby?
- Do I provide myself with the structure I need to work efficiently and effectively?
- Do I treat myself kindly or am I the boss from hell? List some examples.
- Do I think about the future of my business or am I always 'in' my business, doing the day-to-day work?

Remember, this is an audit of your current situation. There is no right or wrong, there is just fact. If you're new to self-employment, and if working from home is a new experience for you, great! You can start as you mean to go on and consider the following points right from day one. If you're more established, then you may need to start breaking a few habits. That's not easy to do, so be a good boss: be kind to yourself, be honest, and take it one step at a time.

What are your 'employee' benefits?

Yes! It's real! You are your own boss so why not make sure your employee benefits are just what you need to be at your very best while you're at work? What a great opportunity to take time to consider what helps you to work well, and to make sure your working day is exactly what you want it to be.

Many microbusiness owners, particularly if you work from home, start off with good intentions but these get brushed to one side when the 'busyness' sets in. I know how easy it can be to ignore what I need in order to fulfil someone else's agenda. I'm not suggesting you turn down paid work. I'm just suggesting that as a microbusiness owner you do have a say in how and when the work gets done.

So, I invite you to consider how you currently treat yourself. Are you being kind to yourself? I have given a few examples below of what floats my business boat to help you get started:

Owl or lark?

Do you know what your natural rhythms are? Most of us are either a night owl – at our best after dark and a bit slow in the mornings – or a lark – alert in the morning and ready for bed well before midnight.

I am most definitely neither! I generally take a few hours to properly wake up, and I love an early night. So, I get up at 6.30am and spend a long time pottering about and having breakfast before walking my dog. I usually start work at about 11am. My working day normally ends at 4pm when I do my grocery shopping, cook dinner and start winding down for the day. I don't work a full day, but the time I spend at my desk is productive and I feel engaged and at my best.

Ask yourself, when am I at my best? Am I currently working with my natural rhythms or fighting against them?

Carrot or stick?

Goal! When you hit your target, complete your tasks, or tick off everything on your to-do list (that will never happen!) how do you reward yourself? Do you give yourself the pat on your back that you deserve?

What do I mean by rewards? Well of course when you've hit some targets and won some lucrative contracts you can go out and buy yourself a flash car and a fortnight in the Maldives. But this is about the daily grind of home working, so the types of rewards I'm talking about are the little ones.

Personally, I like to go for a walk, have a cuppa, play with my dog, and potter in the garden (weather permitting of course). These may be small treats, but they take me away from my desk and give me some breathing space. They're good for me.

Ask yourself, what's good for me? How do I currently thank myself for a job well done?

Exercise or couch potato?

When you work for yourself your level of physical activity can take a nosedive. Maybe you were already the world's worst couch potato, but even driving the car to the office takes up more energy than the stroll from your bedroom down the hall to your home office.

My daily dog walk hits the mark for me. Just stepping outside in the fresh air makes me feel happy and calm and gives me a fresh perspective on my day. I don't fully understand the science behind it, but I know it works.

Ask yourself, is exercise currently a part of my daily routine? What energises me? Is it a priority?

Regular breaks or 'lunch is for wimps'?

According to some macho types, 'lunch is for wimps.' I say working a full day without resting or eating suggests a lack of commitment to your work, as it hinders good concentration and productivity.

If you work from home, it can be easy to work through to 2pm or 3pm without a break simply because you can't tear yourself away. Home working also means however that you do have the opportunity to make the most of being in your own kitchen to prepare food you enjoy.

Food is important to me, and if I don't eat regular healthy meals, I feel the effects physically and emotionally. Eating a shop bought sandwich and drinking a can of pop is OK occasionally but in the long term it isn't sustainable for me. Eating healthy freshly prepared food makes me feel so much better, happier and calmer.

Ask yourself, do I currently eat to nourish and fuel my body? Or do I 'grab and go' from the local shop?

Sofa or desk?

From the very start of my business I have always had a place that I can call my own where I work. A place that is only mine and is away from the daily distractions of life. I like order, and I flourish in a quiet environment.

I do realise however that this doesn't apply to everyone. Some people enjoy the hustle and bustle of a noisy environment and would slowly go mad in a silent room all by themselves. But it is important to be able to work without distraction when you need to, when you have client calls to make for example. You do need a place where you can shut the door if necessary, focus and engage with your business, without the noise of the television, or the chatter of children (easier said than done for some home workers).

Ask yourself, where do I currently work? What does it feel like? Have I got a quiet place where I can focus and be away from daily household distractions?

Dressed or PJs?

Be honest now, would you wear your pyjama bottoms when you're on a video conference? I have been known to, but I couldn't get into the right mindset for the call. How could I when I was wearing my PJs?

This is all about mindset for me. Showering and dressing for the day, whether I'm alone or at a meeting, has a big effect on how professional and capable I feel. It helps me to move my brain from 'home' mode into 'work' mode and creates necessary boundaries which help me focus.

Ask yourself, how do I currently 'appear' at my desk? Am I physically representing how I want to be?

Who is your support network?

I remember my very first day as a self-employed microbusiness owner. I was sat at my desk, tweaking my brand spanking new website (again), and waiting for my phone to ring. I had too many cups of tea to count, and I produced exactly zero amounts of work, I knew no other business owners, and although I had the support from my fantastic husband, I didn't have anyone else to turn to for advice, support or just a plain old 'putting the world to rights' grumble. In fact, and I am trying to remember back here, I don't think I spoke to another human being all day. Now, for me, chatterbox that I am, that is a real achievement!

I can't emphasise enough how important it is to build a network around yourself, that is, if you don't want to go slowly mad and end up having to deal with every little issue in your business all by yourself. Being self-employed, particularly for microbusiness owners who are home based, can be a very solitary and lonely existence, and it takes a huge amount of effort to develop a network around you who are not working as part of your business, but will support you through thick and thin nevertheless.

So, ask yourself, who keeps me sane when the world around me is going mad? Who can I currently turn to when times are tough? Who are my business allies?

What are your superpowers?

Everyone has superpowers. Honestly, I promise, you have superpowers. How exciting is that! All you need to do is cut through the noise of your day to day activities and create some space and time to reflect and you'll soon discover what yours are.

OK, so you don't have to wear your pants outside your trousers, but you will need to start thinking about what's currently great and not so great about you in your business. What are your current strengths and weaknesses? What are your superpowers? What is your super nemesis?

Remember, this is not a 'where you want to be' analysis, it's a 'where you are now' analysis. It's your opportunity to give yourself that pat on the back for all the stuff you do so wonderfully well, and a little nod of acknowledgement for the parts of your development that perhaps you neglect a little.

It's important that you try to be as realistic and precise as you can about your current situation. Be honest with yourself. There are no right or wrong answers. This is yours, it's where you are right now. So, make it work for you.

I thought it would be helpful to share the key questions that I ask myself, along with a few of my answers to get you started. I hope you find this helpful.

Ask yourself:

Q. What am I good at? What are my strengths? What are my superpowers? What comes naturally to me? What do others say they wish they could do as well as me?

A. Delegating work and empowering team members.

Q. What am I not good at? What do I need to improve?

A. I struggle to have potentially confrontational conversations. I get too emotionally embroiled in the situation.

Q. What do I least enjoy doing? What do I put off? Why?

A. Social media marketing. I find it distracting and I don't feel confident in my ability to engage with my audience using social media platforms.

Make a note of your answers in your Thousandaire journal. At this stage I would also encourage you to share your strengths and weaknesses with other people. People you trust and who will have your best interests in mind. Ask them if they agree with your analysis of yourself. How do they experience you? For example, if they work for you and you think you're a great delegator, how do they experience this aspect of you? Do they agree? Or do they think your delegation skills could be improved? Getting feedback in this way can be tough but it will give you more clarity on the reality you're facing.

You'll be thinking about this further in the next chapter when you will start to consider your strengths and weaknesses as a business as well as an individual. But for now, it's just about you.

In summary, this chapter is about you understanding what you need to be the best you can be; it's about being clear about what you are bringing to your business, the good bits and the less good bits; and it's about understanding what changes you may need to make to ensure that you can be the strongest, most confident and competent person you can be.

Everyone will be different and being self-employed is your opportunity to work to all your strengths instead of just some of them. So, I encourage you to take time to consider what makes you strong? Are you treating yourself kindly? Are you embracing and nurturing your superpowers?

What gives you the best chance of being your best you?

Key Points

- Live your values – do your words and actions reflect your values? Are you authentic?

- Be a good boss – would you want to work for you?

- Are you being your best you? Or are you sabotaging yourself and your business?

- Know your personal strengths and weaknesses – bask in the glory of your very own superpowers!

- Who is your support network? Who are your business allies?

Chapter Three
WHERE ARE YOU NOW?
Is your business working for you?

> 'All growth depends upon activity. There is no development physically or intellectually without effort, and effort means work'.
>
> Calvin Coolidge

On your blocks…again…

In the last chapter we talked about what you need to be the best you can be in your business. We considered what you are bringing to your business, good and not so good, and what changes you may want to make to ensure that you are the strongest, most confident and competent person you can be.

This chapter is moving away from you as a business owner and instead focussing on your business itself. The objective is the same though: to encourage you to consider where you are now so you have clarity about what you need to do to move forward. Again, it's about performing an audit of your current reality, but this time on your business instead of on yourself.

By the end of the chapter, you'll have clarity on your current business:

- skills – what are your business strengths and weaknesses?
- finances – what is your lifestyle costing you? How much more do you need?
- business activities – how do you spend your time? Is it profitable?

Remember, each of our businesses will be different, and what you want from your business will be as individual for you as it is for me. There really is no right or wrong here. There's just your current reality. But, if you can consider the current facts of your business, you're one step nearer to making strong and clear decisions on where you want your business to go next. Wherever that is, you will be in control, and I'm sure, like me, you'll want your business to be as strong, confident and competent as you are.

What are your business superpowers?

In the previous chapter we looked at your personal superpowers and super nemesis, your strengths and weaknesses as an individual. This was all in relation to your 'inner world', it was all about you. The next step is to consider the same things but with your 'outer world' in mind.

Just like in the last chapter, you need to create some space and time to reflect on what's great and not so great about your business. What are your current business strengths and weaknesses? What are your business superpowers? What is your business super nemesis?

Don't forget, just as you did with your 'inner world', this is about 'where your business is now'. It's not about 'where you want your business to be'. This is your opportunity to recognise and acknowledge all the amazing work you are doing. It's your chance to spend some time thinking outside your business to the big wide world in which your business exists. What's going on that may impact your business? What opportunities can you find? What's happening that might have a negative impact on your business?

Try to be as realistic and precise as you can about your current situation. Be honest with yourself and your business. Remember, you don't need to fix everything. There will be some issues you'll never be able to fix, you just need to be aware of what's happening within and around your business right now. So, make it work, make it real, and make it make a difference.

So, what do I need to do? I hear you ask? You need to complete a SWOT analysis – I can hear your groans – I'm sorry but it's the only way that you will discover your superpower, and your super nemesis of course, your weaknesses (we all have them) and threats to your business.

So, what is a SWOT analysis?

A SWOT analysis is your opportunity to spend time reflecting on four key areas of your business. These are your strengths - your superpowers, your weaknesses, your opportunities and your threats. Using your Thousandaire journal create your own template by dividing a page into quarters and giving each a heading, like this:

Strengths	Weaknesses
Opportunities	Threats

You have done half of the work already in the previous chapter, so I invite you to pop your 'inner world' strengths and weaknesses into this analysis before you move on.

Below are the key questions that I ask myself, along with a few of the answers from a recent analysis to help you get started. I hope you find this useful.

Strengths

Q. What do you do better than anyone else?
A. Delegate and empower team members.
Q. What is your unique selling point (USP)?
A. The team – Our clients love the fact that they have more than one PA. They have a team supporting them. No other business can offer what we do.
Q. What do other people in your sector see as your strengths?
A. The team – a consistent team that have been working with me for many years.
Q. What advantages do you and your business have?
A. Low overheads. Working from home keeps costs low.

Weaknesses

Q. What could you improve?
A. My ability to have difficult and potentially confrontational conversations.
Q. What loses you sales?
A. Insufficient and haphazard marketing activity.
Q. What do other people in your sector see as your weaknesses?
A. The fact that I offer flexible retainers. I always allow for low and peak seasons for clients.
Q. What do you do a poor job of?
A. I fail to make the effort to understand the big financial picture.

Opportunities

Q. What opportunities do your strengths open you up to?
A. Shout louder about our USP – get the message out there!
Q. What new products or services could you sell?
A. I could choose to use associates that offer services aligned with our core service
Q. What's going on in your sector that you are aware of?
A. Annual Virtual Assistant conferences and awards
Q. What advantages are there in new technology and legislation etc?
A. Keeping on top of new technology will keep my business on top of the game.

Threats

Q. What is your competition doing that you are concerned about?
A. They are very active on social media which is a weak area for me
Q. What threats do your weaknesses expose you to?
A. Potential financial risk as a result of not fully understanding financial reports
Q. What should you be concerned about in the next 6 months?
A. The market is becoming diluted with less qualified and experienced virtual assistants.
Q. What new trends e.g. in technology, are you not making the most of?
A. Instagram

I had a conversation with my accountant when I was writing this chapter and I was reminded that although a SWOT analysis is a useful tool, it's important to remember the point of doing it. What specifically is your objective? The example above is very general and covers your business and you in your business as an entirety.

She suggested that in addition to doing this, and to help drill down to specifics, an analysis of each area of your business would also be useful. You can get even deeper by doing a SWOT on all the specific issues in your original SWOT! Using my example, I could extract my weakness 'I fail to make the effort to understand the big financial picture' and develop a SWOT analysis for this specific issue.

Taking this example a few points of this would be: my strength is that I use cloud accountancy software efficiently to raise invoices, input receipts and reconcile my accounts; my weakness is that I don't fully understand the balance sheet and profit & loss reports; my opportunity is to learn how to create monthly reports showing my big picture and increasing my understanding and control I have over my finances; and my threat is that if I don't do this then something might be going on in my business that will cause problems in the future.

Doing this on a specific area, a weakness in this case, will result in a deeper understanding of the issue, and a list of specific actions that can take place to overcome the weakness. I'll be talking about how to create your action plan and make sure that your actions are SMART (Specific, Measurable, Achievable, Realistic and Timed) in the next chapter.

This same principle could be applied to all aspects of your business.

Once you have your SWOT in place, it's time to reflect upon it. That's also where the deeper insight comes.

As a microbusiness owner, you're never going to be great at everything, but being clear about your strengths, knowing and mitigating against your weaknesses, taking advantage of your opportunities, and understanding the threats you face, will result in you knowing your big picture and being prepared for anything.

So, ask yourself:
- How can I MAKE MORE of my strengths?
- How can I MITIGATE or MINIMISE my weaknesses?
- How can I DEVELOP my opportunities?
- How can I MINIMISE RISKS from my threats?

This is a superpower in itself – the clarity you have from deeply understanding your business and the actions you need to take to improve and protect it into the future. Hopefully you will have glimmers of other potential super powers in your strengths list too.

Don't be afraid of doing a SWOT analysis. It's your friend, embrace it.

Your business finances

Money makes the world go around! Right? Deep down we all know that having a lot of money won't make you happy, but we do need enough money to live the life we want to live. Ideally, we want enough money to not just survive, but to thrive. Think back to your Thousandaire Sweet Spot. What does that look like for you?

As a microbusiness owner, you should feel passionate about what you do, about your business. After all, your business might well be what you spend much of your time doing. But remember, it's not just something you love, it's also something that is paying your bills. You may need your income to pay for all household outgoings, or if you're lucky, you may just need to cover some of them. But when push comes to shove you need your business to provide an income. Otherwise, I'm sorry to say, it's only really a hobby.

What is your lifestyle costing you?

It's important to understand how much money you need to live the life you want. What that life looks like will be different for everyone of course; if you have children they will always need new shoes, school trips etc; if you want to have two exotic holidays a year then you will somehow have to pay for these; if you, like me, enjoy eating out, how much does this cost?

So, what are your finances like? Do you know how much you need to earn to survive? Do you know how much you need to earn to allow you and those closest to you to thrive? Are you anywhere near your Thousandaire Sweet Spot?

It's important to have a clear understanding of your current financial situation, so to help you I have included a simple template to help you assess your outgoings; see the Expenditure chart in the appendix.

This is not a one size fits all template. Every one of you will live different lives with varying priorities and circumstances. But, it's a starter for ten. It gives you some general headings that you can use or tweak to your heart's content. Knowing your outgoings and taking control of them is the first step to financial freedom. You might not like what you find out, you might be pleased with the results, but remember, this is your current situation. Things can only get better from here…

The whole point of this exercise is to discover how much income you need to pay for your lifestyle. After all, what's the point of flogging yourself to death if you can't enjoy a few of the good things in life? Isn't that one of the reasons why you became self-employed in the first place? To give yourself a better work-life balance, to provide you with the lifestyle you want? If this isn't happening, then you need to make some changes. Instead of reducing your expenditure, although you might need to do this in the short term, you need to increase your business income. You need to make your business work harder on your behalf.

Is your business working for you?

Is your business working for you? Or are you working for your business?

Hopefully you will have shouted a resounding 'yes' to the first question. Ideally, your business will be generating an income without you. Now, I do understand that you might be new to this 'Thousandaire' malarkey, and that many of you might not yet be at that stage. However, there are a few areas that you might want to consider right now to help you assess your current business circumstances.

How do you spend your time?

No matter where you're working or who you're working for, you need structure in your working day. When you work for a company, this comes naturally – you have your start and finish times, your lunch breaks (if you're lucky these days!) and your boss managing what you do.

When you're running your own business from home, it's no different. You have the flexibility to set your own hours and work when you like, but you still need to make sure you know what you are going to spend your time on. Being your own boss means doing all the things for yourself a boss would normally do for you – so you need to manage yourself and your own hours.

Consider how much time you currently spend on the following:

- **Paid work**

Whether you produce widgets or provide a service the work that brings in the money is the bread and butter of your business. This will vary depending on whether you work alone or you have a team supporting you.

- **Unpaid work**

Time spent managing your business: doing your bookkeeping, answering emails, networking, marketing, recruiting, strategy and business planning, such as doing your SWOT analysis.

- **Wasted time**

Time spent faffing about doing nothing. I know you do it, because we all do it! It's not all wasted time, some of it is time to think and regroup, but too much of this and nothing will get done. Social media can be a deadly enemy here! Or if you're working from home, suddenly having an urgent need to do the ironing rather than tackle a chewy business problem.

I have found it useful to log my time 'live' to see how much time I spend on each area of my business. This will give you an accurate account of

your time worked each day and an insight into how productive you are. I encourage you to do this for a few weeks to get a good indication of what you are spending your time doing, or not doing! You can use a free online system, such as Toggl (www.toggl.com), a spreadsheet, or simply take your Thousandaire journal and list the hours of the day in 15-minute blocks. Then make a note of what you're doing in each block.

Once you've done this spend a few minutes really considering the results. Has anything surprised you? Is your time productive? What could you do differently?

Having this information at your fingertips will be important when you decide to start growing your business. There are a few different growth models and I will be talking about some of these in the next chapter, with a particular focus on the Thousandaire model of course!

Is your business profitable?

I know from bitter experience how easy it can be to spend my time on things I enjoy doing, rather than on things that I should be doing. It's called procrastination, and I'm an effortless expert in this! Especially as a lone home worker, it can be easy to spend all day 'playing' at being in business, instead of focussing on the nuts and bolts of being in business – making a profit!

Following on from the exercise above, I encourage you to consider whether your business is focussing on profitable activities. If it's currently just you in your business, is your time being spent on productive and profitable work? Or are you messing about in the background, like I was, being busy but unproductive?

I invite you to look over your records for the past twelve months (or six if you've not been in business that long). Twelve months will enable you to see if your profit relates to seasons or behaviours across the year. For example, if you're in swimwear retail, you're likely to see peaks in sales in the summer months. If you're providing a business service, such as marketing, you might notice trade goes down in the summer months when many people are on holiday.

Ask yourself:

- What areas of my business are the most profitable?
- What areas of my business are the least profitable?
- What product or service brings in the most profit?
- What product or service, if any, could I stop providing?
- What new products or services could I introduce that would be profitable?

What is the cost of your service or product?

It's important as you grow your Thousandaire business to make sure that what you are charging your clients and customers covers your costs and pays you enough money to thrive (Remember your Thousandaire Sweet Spot).

Consider what you are currently charging. Have you researched the market rate of what you offer? What do your competitors charge? Where do you currently sit on the pricing scale? Are you cheap or expensive or somewhere in between? Have you reviewed your prices since you started?

It's easy when you first start out to think that you need to keep your prices low to encourage business, but the negative impact of this can be three-fold:

You might be keeping the market value of your product or service low for yourself and for everybody else.

It's always hard to increase your price in the future. It's much easier to go in high from the start and sell your service based on added value and unique selling points.

When you start building your team you won't be able to pay them. Simple. Unless your prices are high enough you won't have any flexibility around paying for the team that are going to help your business to grow.

Outsourcing – expense or investment?

So, you should have a good idea now what you are spending your time doing, and what areas of your business are most profitable. It's at this stage, when you need to consider outsourcing some of your work to somebody else. Scary stuff eh? Will they be good enough? How much will it cost? Nobody will do it as well as I can? These are all legitimate fears, but fears don't have to become reality. With the right research, and the right people, outsourcing is your way to increased profit.

Consider what you are currently spending your time doing. If it's not profitable, could you be outsourcing it? For example, you can't raise an invoice for your time spent creating the perfect website (unless you're a website company that is). You could pay someone else to build your website but of course that will come at a cost. But consider the cost of doing it yourself: the weeks of your time; the sweat on your brow;

the skills you'll have gained that you'll never need again; the fact that you can't charge anybody for your time, skills or sweat – remember, no charge equals no profit.

In my opinion, outsourcing is an investment in your future. When somebody else is building your website, you could be creating value in your product or service, you could be raising invoices!

It often transpires that outsourcing is an indirect way of building genuine business relationships. If you outsource your website development to a professional who also builds websites for other businesses, they will get to know you, what you do and what you stand for. And there is every chance they will refer and recommend you if relevant clients and customers show up. The more people you connect with, the more opportunity you will have to help people through your business.

So, consider what you are currently outsourcing. Are you doing everything yourself? If so, you're not going to just start outsourcing all your non-profitable work straight away, but at this stage it's a good idea to start thinking about it.

Ask yourself, if I could lose one thing from my to do list, what would it be?

How much money are you wasting?

When was the last time you looked in detail at your business expenses? What are you currently paying for that you no longer need? List all your business expenses and consider how necessary or smart they are. This isn't a trigger to stop outsourcing if you already are! But it is about critically analysing the value of everything you're paying for – the value to your well-being and your business. Often, we find we are paying for subscriptions, memberships and training we simply no longer need or make use of, or we haven't shopped around to get the best deal.

I remember doing this for the first time and discovering that I was paying more for my insurance than a friend who ran a similar business. I was also paying for a mobile phone contract that had long since run out and I hadn't got around to replacing my phone. So, in a couple of days I had saved money on my insurance and upgraded my phone – result!

Every business, however small, will have expenses, but take some time to have a long hard look at what you are currently paying for. Can you switch providers? Are there expenses that you had forgotten about, and you can now cancel? Are you getting best value for money?

Remember, every penny saved is a penny added to your bottom line. In other words, it's more profit. And as my Mum always says, 'look after the pennies and the pounds look after themselves'. Wise words Mum, thank you.

What is your buffer?

Whatever your circumstances, if you are going to relinquish some of your income to outsource work, you still need to be able to pay your household bills. Just because you are on your journey to becoming a Thousandaire, doesn't mean that the utility companies and your mortgage provider will be joining you on your journey. Unfortunately, they will still want to be paid. This is a sad fact of life.

You may well already have the mindset of a Thousandaire, but you still need to pay your bills and part of your planning is to consider who will support you during your time of frugality as you transition to a Thousandaire business model. What is your plan? Do you have savings you can dip into? Do you have a supportive partner? Do you have a secondary income stream you could set up temporarily, such as letting a room in your house to a lodger?

Once you know what your personal circumstances are you can plan and adjust the pace of your rise to Thousandaire status accordingly.

I was lucky enough to have a husband who encouraged my enthusiasm and who worked hard to ensure that we could still eat. Having said that, my business growth was deliberately slow and organic, and I was in no rush to outsource my work all at once, so my financial risk felt under control and manageable.

You are your own boss here remember and it is only you who will dictate the pace of growth, and it is only you who will know the value of that financial risk. I would recommend you doing a quick calculation of how much money you need to survive for a year if you don't get any work in at all. Ask yourself, what is my worst-case scenario?

This chapter is all about checking how sustainable your business is. Are you flogging a dead horse? That might sound a bit harsh but in simple terms are you making enough money to thrive rather than just survive? If not, have your findings given you any ideas of where you can make changes – what activities you can do more of, and which ones to drop?

How healthy is your business? Is it doing what you want it to do? Is it being what you want it to be?

Checking all these things from time to time is critical to your business growth. It can be easy to let things slip, and at the end of the day if something isn't working it needs to be changed. And planning for change is where we're heading in the next chapter.

Key Points

- Know your business superpowers and super nemesis – drill down into the specifics as that is where your real powers lay

- Understand what your lifestyle is costing you – what can you change?

- Know your financial buffer – how much money do you need for your first year if you don't earn anything?

- Consider how you spend your time – what are your priorities?

- Think about what business activities are the most profitable – can you do more of this?

Chapter Four
WHERE DO YOU WANT TO BE?

> 'Just don't give up trying to do what you really want to do. Where there is love and inspiration, I don't think you can go wrong.'
> Ella Fitzgerald

Do you remember your Thousandaire Sweet Spot? We talked about it in Chapter One. You spent time considering the million-dollar question: what's enough for you? Enough money, enough time, enough energy, enough of the good stuff in life that feeds our souls as well as our wallets. In other words, what do you want your life to look like?

As microbusiness owners what your life looks like will very much depend on what your business looks like, and how you function within your business. So, before you move forward with this chapter you might find it useful to refresh yourself on Chapter One and your responses.

Take some time to return to your vision and remind yourself about where you want to be and what success looks like for you. It's important to get clarity on this now, as this chapter is about taking the first steps toward making your vision your reality. It's about getting to grips with how you are going to grow your business and ultimately how your business is going to look. More than that, we're going to start thinking about how to set some clear goals to help you get there.

I'm going to outline the different microbusiness growth models you may want to consider. The rest of this book is all about The Thousandaire Model, because it's how I grew my business and what I love, but it's certainly not the only way to build a sustainable, scalable business.

Remember that your future success should be about what you want to achieve and not what others think you should be achieving. The growth model you choose (and hopefully, as you're reading this book it will be The Thousandaire Model!) is your decision, and yours alone. After all, there is no one size fits all solution. Having these options laid out and making a clear decision on how to move forward at this stage will save you a lot of time and energy in the future.

By the end of the chapter, you'll be able to identify:

- your business growth model of choice
- how to start planning and thinking about your goal setting journey

So, what growth models am I talking about? I'm sure they've all got their proper names but as you may know by now, theory is not my strong point! I've called these models just as I see them so here goes…

Outsource the things you don't know how to do (or you don't enjoy doing)

This model keeps you right in the centre of things when it comes to what your business does. You will focus on what you do well, providing your service or making your product, and you will eventually outsource everything else.

Most of us microbusiness owners start off by doing everything ourselves. We run the business, we do our own marketing, design our own website, reconcile our own books, the list goes on…we also work on behalf of our clients and customers. Very quickly we can become a Jack of all trades, juggling multiple tasks and skills but not actually doing a brilliant job at many of them, especially the jobs that we are figuring out as we go along.

With this model, you will keep on doing what you do best, and in time, as finances allow, outsource everything else.

Outsourcing the jobs that require a specialist, instead of spending weeks trying to figure out how to do it yourself, is a great option for growing your business. You'll be able to focus on what you do best. You'll have the time to give 100% of your attention to your customers, enhancing your service or product and offering the very best value. Most probably, you'll enjoy your business more too, which will be reflected in your work and customer relationships. So, it's a sound business decision.

The down side of this model is that your business growth will still be based around the number of hours available to you and the market value of your product or service. Once you've hit the ceiling on both you'll have nowhere else to go.

The good news is, this model is compatible with the others too – so if finances allow, why not have the best of both worlds?!

Diversification

This model provides your clients with a route to other service providers that offer complementary expertise. It allows you to offer a full suite of services to clients, rather than just your product or service. All offerings are marketed under the same brand umbrella, but the umbrella is bigger and more diverse. An example of this would be a marketing consultancy adding social media and copywriting to its list of services, or a virtual assistant company, like mine, offering telephone answering or bookkeeping services. The important thing here is to ask yourself 'does it make sense to my clients to offer these new services'? If your answer is 'yes' then perhaps this would be a good growth strategy for you.

The key benefit of this model is that your clients will have a one stop shop for any services that are associated with your key offering. This makes their life easier, and people are happy to pay for convenience.

In my opinion however, this is a tricky model to control. How do you know if what your associates are providing is good enough? You don't offer the same service as them and you don't fully understand what they do, so how can you ensure that what they are doing is maintaining your high standards. How do you manage your quality control?

In addition to this, as the brand ambassador, you will be responsible for setting contracts or working agreements with your associates as well as your clients, invoicing your clients, paying your associates and dealing with any complaints and/or financial hiccups. This can become a tricky area to navigate. Make sure you have total clarity over who does what, how the financials are going to work and who ultimately is responsible to the client for the work done.

Another word of advice when it comes to diversification. I have so often seen business owners promoting a service or product that has nothing to do with what they've become known for. For example, one minute they are promoting their life coaching business and suddenly they start selling products through a network marketing company. Now, there is nothing wrong with either, and it's fine to have side projects, but you need to consider the message this gives to your potential customers.

Whenever I have come across this it leaves me feeling confused about what they do, where their attention is going, what their expertise is, and it shouts out to me that their main business is not doing very well. This may not be true, but is that what you want people to think?

Create a product from your 1:1 service that you can sell to many

More and more microbusiness owners are creating value in what they do by developing a product that can be sold multiple times i.e. an online course or group programme. These are often delivered using videos or workbooks. An example of this would be a lifestyle coach who previously offered a 1:1 coaching session, deciding to develop a coaching video that can be sold multiple times. So, instead of being restricted by time, they can do the work once and then promote and sell it as many times as they want.

This model can make the service or product more accessible to potential clients. A video, for example, can be offered at a lower price than a 1:1 session, and can be done at the client's own pace.

There are two main things to consider when deciding if this is for you. Firstly, can your product or service be delivered to a high standard in a group or self-study way? This may work for some businesses but not others – for example, a virtual assistant business would struggle to offer a group service, unless they were providing productivity tips and accountability, rather than doing the work.

And secondly, does it play to your strengths as a business owner? Look back to the work you did on your SWOT in the previous chapter. Also, if, like me, you value strong and close relationships with your clients, this model may take you away from that.

The Thousandaire Model

Yay! This is the model that I love! It's how I have grown my business, and as the title of this book suggests, it's how I have developed a lifestyle that feeds into my Thousandaire Sweet Spot!

So, what is the Thousandaire model? The primary aim of this model is to increase your income potential by releasing you from the restrictions of working on a time basis. You'll be outsourcing all your key business offerings, what your business does, what you are skilled at, and what your customers pay for.

That doesn't mean you're not involved in your business, you absolutely are, and you should be, but mainly you'll be managing and growing your team, finding new clients and planning your next growth spurt. It's about becoming a leader of your business, not working in it all the time.

The Thousandaire model is about finding trusted associates who can replicate what you do and allow you to increase your client base beyond your personal capacity.

How to build a time machine

Imagine having a time machine – you could work for a client all day and then go back and do it all over again for another client, then again, and again, until your productivity and earning potential reached your wildest dreams. You would be exhausted of course, and nothing much else would be happening in your life (remember the gloomy prediction at my first networking experience?), but your bank balance would look extremely healthy. Or, you could build a team around you that would effectively do the same thing with a lot less effort from you. Sounds good doesn't it? Your very own time machine, without all the travelling backwards and forwards in time of course.

OK, so I've highlighted the downside of all the other growth models I've talked about, so I think it's fair to do the same here. Let's talk about how you pay for all these trusted associates…

The Financial Tipping Point

I remember the first time I gave client work to an associate. I had mixed feelings about it. Feelings of fear and excitement – excitement about running a business with more than one person in it, and fear over whether they would let both myself and my client down. A real mixed emotional bag, and one which I often think back on whenever I am tempted back to working with clients myself.

I was lucky. My first associate was, and still is, fabulous, and my clients were very happy with the work that was produced. Phew!

Then the inevitable happened, and I received an invoice from my associate. That can't be right, can it? I get someone else to do the work and then I need to pay them? Surely not! I know it sounds simple, because it is simple, but when you start to outsource work to others, your income will reduce significantly. And it's tough, believe me, it's very tough.

I am sure you loved the idea of having a time machine when you read it, but the downfall, and it's a biggie, is that you need to pay for all the work that is done on your behalf. That's right, you will no longer get to keep all the money that your clients pay you!

This can be a tricky and scary time for a microbusiness owner, but in my experience, you need to ride this financial storm before you can reap the rewards.

The See Saw Effect

Imagine you have one person on either side of a see saw. You have a fabulous balance, right? You on one end, and a client on the other. Everyone is happy and you are being paid for the work you have done.

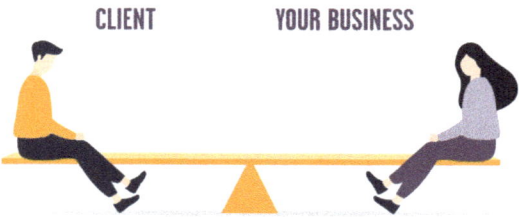

Now, imagine adding another person on the seat with you. Suddenly everything is out of kilter and your one client now must support both of you financially. Your income stays the same but there are now two of you to support.

What you need to do is put another client on the see saw with you. Then another, then another and then another. Ultimately with you working on the strategic development of the business and with your growing team working on the front line, you will be able to re-create that balance and in time tip the see saw in the opposite direction.

In other words, once you are no longer working on direct client or customer work, the more clients you get the less risk you take on. That is the financial tipping point. It will be different for every business and it is worth taking the time to map it out for yours.

This is where you need to look at the numbers and the detail. If you were to start small and take on one associate, how much would you pay them, and what other costs do you need to consider? Once you have that figure, work out how many new clients you need to cover the cost (and then some).

Here are a few examples of the sort of thing you might want to consider:

- How much are you going to pay your team members? What is the industry rate? Is this a viable cost for your business? Are you looking for cheap and cheerful or highly skilled and expensive? What do you need to pay to maintain your high standards?

- How much does it cost to recruit a new team member? How much is your time worth? How much do the contracts cost? Do you need outside expertise to help with recruitment, for example psychometric testing and help with interviewing?

- What's the costs of the tools and technology that you may need to provide so they can work effectively?
- How much will you spend on team perks, for example, the Christmas party?
- What is the cost of staff turnover? If a team member leaves what financial implications will this have for you? How will you fill the gap?

You need to always remember your vision and your big picture at this stage otherwise you may be tempted to flounder and take a backward step. Remember, everything you pay to your team is an investment in the long-term financial stability of your business. There is no gain without a little pain first.

It's a goal!

You now have your vision, you know your values, you've considered what your superpowers are, and you have hopefully decided to become a Thousandaire. Brilliant!

So, what next? The key now is to work smarter and not harder. You need to understand how to set yourself goals and how to create an action plan and task list which will take you step by step and day by day to where you want to be.

The psychological effect of setting a goal can't be underestimated. Once you have a goal, you know where you're going, what work you need to do, what steps you must take to get there and what challenges you will need to overcome along the way.

Don't worry, you don't have to set any goals, at least not right now, but I thought it would be useful to share a few of the tools that I use to help me keep my business on track. Having a 'goal mindset' at this stage will help you as you progress further into the book, and I will be asking you to refer to this section from time to time, so you might want to make a note of your initial thoughts and ideas in your Thousandaire journal.

Plan your ascent

I was introduced into the concept of having a 'goal mountain' many years ago and I absolutely love the way it visually depicts what I am trying to achieve. Here's how it looks:

Consider if you're goal was to reach the summit of Everest. You wouldn't just stand at the bottom of the mountain and start walking. Each stage of your ascent is a goal, and each stage of that goal becomes an action. You would break it down into small manageable steps.

You can build your goals into a plan for the day ahead, the week, a year or longer if you want. It's all about having a vision and exercising a bit of control over how your time and energy is spent.

Make your mountain a SMART mountain

Every stage on your ascent is an action and if you're serious about ticking off your action list and reaching your goals, every action should be SMART.

S for Specific

For example, 'be a successful business owner' is not specific enough. How are you defining that success? Break it down as much as possible – a better goal would be 'to have three more clients by the end of the month', for example. This brings you to set more goals leading you to achieve that – more networking, for example, a marketing push, or introducing a referral system for existing clients.

M for Measurable

Facts, figures and evidence are what is needed here. The example above is ideal – it's quite difficult to be woolly over how many clients you have! Also, you need to know when you have achieved the goal, otherwise how will you know when it's time to crack open that bottle of bubbly?

A for Achievable

'Make a million in a year' is not a SMART goal for most of us. Aim high but if that's all you have on your to-do list when you sit at your desk in the mornings, you're probably going to feel a bit overwhelmed. Once again, break it down. Work back from your final goal if you need to and figure out all the steps you need to take to get you there. Each one of those steps is a goal – it needs to be properly set, worked towards, and celebrated once you've achieved it.

R for Realistic for you

Remember to make sure that your goal is something that you are both willing and able to work toward. There is no point in setting a goal that you are never going to achieve. Nobody else is setting these goals for you so you can control what they are and how quickly you achieve them.

T for Timed

There's nothing like a deadline to get you motivated. Be realistic about how long tasks will take and give yourself enough time to do them. The advantages of being your own boss is that you don't have to drive yourself to meet impossible targets any more. And if you can score your goal ahead of schedule then do what any decent boss would do – give yourself the afternoon off!

'To-do or not to-do?' That is the question!

For many of us, having a to-do list can be the number one reason for things NOT being done. It's easy to become so overwhelmed by the number of things on your list that you can feel stuck in your own business; unable to move forward because you can't see the wood for the trees. There's just too much to do!

Do you remember how your to-do list first started?

Perhaps the list started off with a few scribbles that may have included "call Sue" or "send leaflet & business card to Bob". As your day went on, you may have added a few more things such as "remember dry cleaning" or "send out monthly invoices".

Sometime over the next day, you remember that you haven't got around to speaking to that web designer you met last week so you scrawl "do website" on your list. And before you know it, your to-do list has filled a whole A4 piece of paper decorated with post-it notes for added effect.

This kind of to-do list is going to be a weight around your shoulders. It's the kind that gives you a constant nagging guilt that only reminds you how inefficient you are and how much you still need to squeeze into your working day.

This is NOT how a to-do list should be!

A to-do list should simply be a list of things that need doing sometime in the next few hours. It shouldn't include things such as "do website" or "sort out customer database" on it. These are projects which need planning and scheduling.

There is absolutely no reason why your to-do list shouldn't have a maximum of 6 things listed; half a dozen actions that are small enough to fit in to your working day.

You see, most of the things on your to-do list are probably not to-dos at all - they are projects and actions that can be planned in to your diary or delegated out for others to do.

A popular and useful tool for helping to prioritise and reduce your to-do list is Steven Covey's Quadrants (outlined in the classic '7 Habits of Highly Effective People'). This model encourages you to consider the urgency and importance of each item on your to-do list as the following diagram demonstrates:

	URGENT	**NOT URGENT**
IMPORTANT	*Urgent & important* This stuff needs to be done now!	*Not urgent but important* These tasks can be planned and diarised.
NOT IMPORTANT	*Urgent but not important* You shouldn't be doing this work, it's not important! Who else can do this for you?	*Not urgent and not important* Why is this on your list?

This is easy enough to do, but as usual I like to keep things as uncomplicated and as simple as possible, so I want to show you what I do on a regular basis. It's called the 4 Ds model, and along with a lot of other people I know, I find this to be the most straightforward way to prioritise what I need to do on any specific day.

Step 1 - Take your to-do list, as it stands right now. Bring together all your post it notes, scribbles, lists from your phone or computer etc into one place.

Step 2 - draw a big square on a piece of paper and divide into 4 boxes and label the boxes as follows:

DO IT!	**DATE IT!**
It's urgent and important so what are you waiting for? DO IT!	It's important but not urgent so stick it in your diary!
DELEGATE IT!	**DUMP IT!**
It's urgent but not important so get someone else to do it!	It's not urgent and it's not important so ask yourself – why is this on my to do list?

Step 3 – Fill it in

Now you can't get easier than that can you? So, go and grab your to-do list right now and decide which box each item should be listed in.

The only things that should be going into the DO IT box are the things that are urgent and important. For example, "return customer call who hasn't received confirmation for a workshop tomorrow" or "call customer whose credit card payment has not been approved."

I can guarantee that at least 80% of your to-do list will fit into the DATE IT box. Yup, you've guessed it! This is the box for everything that can be planned. Things like "do website" and "send out monthly invoices" can be scheduled into your diary, either as a planning or an activity session. And by taking the time out to plan something like "do website", you will realise that there are far smaller and easier steps to take to help you complete this project.

The two lower boxes are my favourite. Delegate anything that is not important to you but urgent to your business and dump anything that is, quite frankly, neither important nor urgent, to either you or your business.

As your business grows, you will find that the examples used above for the DO IT box can easily be moved in to the DELEGATE IT box and be delegated to someone else. So, in theory, you should never have a to-do list - only delegated tasks and projects to manage.

How does your to-do list make you feel now?

Hopefully you will now know which model you are going to use to grow your business. Do you want to be a Thousandaire? Or would you prefer to follow a different model? Either way, I would encourage you to continue reading as although this book is all about becoming a Thousandaire, much of what I talk about in the next few chapters will also apply to other growth models.

You should also by now understand the goal mindset and how to set SMART goals which are broken down into achievable bite sized to-do lists that work with you instead of against you.

But what about the detail of making it happen? How do you need to go about it? What skills do you need to do it successfully? That's where we turn next.

Key Points

- Be clear about which growth model is best for you. Having this clarity will provide you with better direction

- Understand your financial tipping point – map it out for your business. What does it look like?

- Investigate the costs of taking on an associate. How much will you pay them? What other legal and business costs are involved?

- Work smarter instead of harder – plan the ascent of your SMART mountain

- Understand the difference between urgent and important. Create a to-do list that works for you.

Chapter Five

GETTING READY:
Mindset & Behaviours

> 'Whether you think you can or whether you
> think you can't, you're right.'
> Henry Ford

Wow! We're storming ahead and you're well on your way to becoming a fully-fledged Thousandaire. That's fantastic! Before you read on though, I would like to invite you to take a moment to reflect on what you have done so far, to acknowledge your progress, and to congratulate yourself on a job well done. Believe me, every step you take, however small, is a step toward your dreams, and at this stage on your journey you've really come a long way, so give yourself a pat on the back, take a deep breath and then keep going…

How to 'Be' a Thousandaire

If you remember, Chapter Two was all about placing your feet firmly on your starting blocks. It was about finding a clear focus on your current 'inner world' situation so that you can effectively move forward. Remember, your 'inner world' isn't about your business assets and tactics, it's about you as an integral part of your business, your mindset, your behaviours and your personal strengths and weaknesses.

Yes, the Thousandaire model is about successfully growing your business so that you no longer work on the front line. But it also goes a lot deeper than that. It's about having clear values, it's about acting in a way that reflects your values to everyone around you, it's about discovering a lifestyle that fulfils and motivates you, and it's about being kind to yourself. It's about walking the walk, being authentic, and 'being' a Thousandaire right down to your very core.

In this chapter I'll be talking about the detail of making that happen, giving you tools and strategies to help you along the way, and helping you to unwrap your skills so that you can do it successfully. I'll be delving once again into your inner world and giving you an insight into how to 'be' a Thousandaire.

Don't worry, I'll be talking more about your actual business in Chapter Six, but for now it's all about you, so sit back, grab a cuppa and once again make yourself the centre of your own universe, at least for now anyway.

By the end of the chapter, you'll have a better understanding of:

- how to put yourself in your business driving seat
- how to develop healthy boundaries
- how to overcome your 'What if Monster'
- how to be more accountable to yourself
- how to make sure you end your day on a high

I want to emphasise at this stage that you probably won't read this chapter and suddenly become a different person, the perfect microbusiness owner. It has taken me years to understand how important these things are, and although I now truly understand their value, I still don't always get it right.

Understanding is your first step though, then it's all about trying them out and seeing how they impact on how you are in your business, and how they affect the results you get. The more you practice the easier it will become and ultimately it will become second nature. That's my plan anyway!

Are you in the driving seat?

Do you ever find yourself saying yes to something that you know you don't want to do? Have you ever heard the word 'yes' coming out of your mouth when inside you're screaming 'no!'?

When I first set up in business, I was guilty of saying yes to all sorts of things that I knew deep down were wrong for me and for my business. In hindsight, I can only put it down to desperation. I was desperate for business, I was desperate for money, and I was desperate to please my clients, whatever the cost to me. Personally, I find it particularly difficult to say no because at my core I'm a people pleaser, I like everyone around me to be happy, and sometimes that can be at my expense.

It was a long time before I understood the reality of what I was doing to myself. I slowly realised that by saying yes to someone else meant I was often saying no to myself. I needed to turn the tables. Instead of grabbing every opportunity, I needed to balance my needs with the needs of everyone else.

It's a tough thing to do for many people, especially if you're working from home. Interruptions and requests can come from all directions. It might be a business request, or it might be an interruption from family. Whatever it is, it's interrupting your space, your thinking and your work-flow.

Imagine a day when you have planned to achieve a certain amount of work, or you're working to a tight deadline, or perhaps you have planned to have the day off. Whatever your personal objectives for that day, when you're interrupted by a request from someone else, you need to be able to actively reflect and respond in a way that keeps everyone happy, including you.

Saying yes to something that isn't right for you will also potentially have a huge impact on your business. If you get offered some work that you know isn't right for you, maybe it's not your niche market, or perhaps it's work that you don't particularly enjoy doing, saying yes will only result in you not being able to take on other work that is perfect for you.

It's very easy, particularly when you're newly self-employed, to grab every opportunity like it's going to be your last. Like I talked about earlier, it's so easy to feel desperate in the early days, but, and it's a big but, all you will be doing is saying no to the head-space, time and opportunity for developing the work you really want to do. Work that moves your vision forwards instead of backwards, work that enhances rather than restricts your business.

Here are my top tips on successfully saying yes to yourself:

Don't answer straight away

Even if you are being asked a direct question that makes you feel like you should say yes. Take a step back, give yourself some breathing space. Whatever you do, don't let anyone make you feel pressurised to answer right away.

Give yourself the time and space to think it through

Give yourself the physical, mental and emotional space to really think about how you are going to answer. Does it align with your business goals and vision? Do you want to do it? Do you have the skills and the time? Or will it leave you feeling stressed and anxious about possibly under-performing or letting people down?

Be calm, be kind and be understanding

If you want to say no, say no! You can be calm, you can be kind, and you can be understanding of what that person might need, but even though they might need it, you don't have to do it. Remember, saying no to them is saying yes to yourself.

Practice makes perfect

Practice it with those closest to you. I promise you with a little practice you'll get so good at doing this.

I'm not saying that you should always say no, sometimes we say yes because it just feels right, or because you really want to help regardless of what you might need. What I am saying is that giving yourself the space and time to actively reflect on the request will leave you in the driving seat instead of in the metaphorical boot!

Know your boundaries

There will always be people who don't respect your boundaries and who will again and again have unreasonable expectations on your time, space and energy. As a microbusiness owner, you need to establish clear boundaries, or you will never get anything done.

It's important to remember that you should set your own boundaries. Don't allow other people to impose their boundaries upon you. Remember, it's all part of learning to say no to other people so that you can say yes to yourself.

If you are working from home and your children are around, then you may enjoy being interrupted every five minutes, or you may not. If a client is phoning you at 10pm just after you've got ready for bed, you may be fine with that, or you may not. It's up to you to decide how important these interruptions are and whether you are willing to tolerate and accept them.

You may want to consider the following:

- What are your standard working days and hours?
- What is and what isn't an emergency? This is particularly important if you have family wanting your attention.
- How will you set client expectations? It's always better to under promise and over deliver than the other way around.
- What are your own boundaries around checking email and social

media accounts etc?

- What are your non-negotiables? For example, what do you need to do for yourself each day to function well (e.g. how much sleep/fresh air/exercise do you want to build in?)

What I am saying here is that by considering, setting and communicating your boundaries you will provide some clarity over what is and what is not acceptable to you and to everyone around you. It makes life more straightforward for everyone and it puts you once again firmly in the driving seat.

What if you fly?

> There is freedom waiting for you,
> on the breezes of the sky,
> and you ask, "what if I fall"?
> Oh, but my darling,
> what if you fly?
>
> ~ Eric Hanson~

I love this poem! It sums up much of what I believe in life. What if you fly? What if you could overcome your self-doubt and fear of falling and fly?

Since becoming self-employed I have spoken to so many microbusiness owners who struggle with being loud and proud about their business. Their fear of standing up and being seen in the big bad world of sales and marketing can be a huge barrier to their business growth.

If you used to work for a large organisation you probably took for granted how fantastic the sales and marketing departments were. In most cases you probably didn't even recognise their existence – unless you used to work in that area of course. Now you're self-employed you no longer have a professional sales and marketing team behind you selling your services or products, shouting from the rooftops about how amazing you are.

Once I became self-employed, I soon recognised what a fantastic job they did. Suddenly I was having to produce all my own marketing material – website, flyers, business cards etc, as well as having to come to terms with talking to people about what I do – and having a 60 second elevator pitch – scary stuff!

Let's face it though, as microbusiness owners, self-promotion is just a fact of life. We have no choice but to do it if we want our potential clients to know who we are, what we do and that we have arrived. If we want to be visible and grow, we quite simply need to self-promote. So, why does it make many of us want to run and hide? Why don't we do it? After all, you only need to talk about your business. You think it's great so surely everyone else will too?

Sounds easy doesn't it? Well I have learned over the years that it most certainly is not easy. Putting your heart and soul 'out there' is a really hard thing to do. It feels scary. What if they don't like me? What if I make a fool of myself? What if my product or service isn't as good as I think it is? What if I embarrass myself? These are all questions that our subconscious mind asks to try and stop us moving forward. They can put a total halt to our marketing activities as fear grips us. Fear of what might happen – and trust me we always seem to think the worst of ourselves.

I call this inner critic my 'WHAT IF MONSTER'

You need to slay your monster – it is after all only in your head and at this point you are making up horror stories to prevent you from doing something that you are perceiving to be hard.

A very wise woman said to me once (thank you Jules Wyman) 'If you're going to make shit up, make up good shit'. And she's right, why would you make up a horror story when you can make up a love story instead? It's because we're all too often hard wired to think the worst of ourselves.

I struggled with this for years. Not moving forward because I feared what might happen if I put myself 'out there'. I have learned though that it really doesn't have to be that way. It is possible to feel good about self-promotion and use it to successfully attract new clients and find new opportunities for ourselves.

Try the following exercise:

Next time you find yourself paralysed by your What If Monster, try fighting back by flipping your negative statement into a positive statement and then stop for a minute and consider the difference and how the positive question makes you feel.

For example:

NEGATIVE QUESTIONS	POSITIVE QUESTION
What if people don't like me?	What if people really like me? How will I feel then?
What if I embarrass myself?	What if I do a great job? How will I feel then?
What if my product isn't as good as I think it is?	What if my product is a huge success? How will I feel then?

So, it's about turning it from a negative to a positive and then thinking about how that is going to make you feel. With this book, I could have asked myself 'what if nobody buys it?' but instead I asked myself 'what if they do?!' How will that make me feel, how proud will I be of myself?

Trust me when I say that I know how hard this can be, but the more you focus on positive outcomes the more confident you will become, and the more your business will grow.

It's not all about you...

Another useful trick is to change the emphasis on self-promotion and focus on trying to make your work visible instead. I think the word 'self' is a big part of the problem as it creates a personal angle to what we are doing. This can make us feel like we are bragging or selfish or being too pushy. But it's not all about you! It's about your business and the service or product that you provide.

So, don't talk about you. Talk about how your product or service makes a difference. Just make your work visible. Now doesn't that already sound like an easier prospect?

- Stop thinking of promoting your business and start focussing on being of service to your customers.
- Stop thinking about what it is you do and start focussing on how your work and your skills and experience can help other people.

In other words, start thinking about your business from your customers perspective and provide them with what they need – not what you want to sell.

Imagine how amazing it would be to have a conversation with someone about how your business can solve their problems without your inner 'What if Monster' popping up telling you that you're going to do it all wrong? Instead, you will have straight forward and honest conversations with a clear focus on how you can be of service.

How refreshing would that be?

Be a good friend to yourself

How would you talk to yourself as a child? Would you berate yourself? Would you tell yourself that you can't possibly achieve what you want to achieve? Or, would you tell yourself how amazing you are, to reach for the moon and that anything is possible if you work hard enough?

We're very good at being unkind to ourselves, and at finding reasons not to move forward, but when you're struggling with self-doubt or your What If Monster, talk to yourself as you would to a child. I'm pretty sure that most of the time you will be kind and compassionate, encouraging and positive.

It works in the same way when we talk to a close friend. We're always compassionate and encouraging. We would never tell them that they were rubbish or that they didn't deserve to do well. Would we? I certainly wouldn't!

So, I encourage you to find either a photo of yourself as a young child or a photo of a friend, keep it on your desk, and when your What If Monster rears its head, talk to the person in the photo. What would you say?

Be accountable

Being accountable is critical to growing a business, any business, and indeed any plan or project you can think of requires you to be accountable to someone. It may be someone else or it may be you but either way being accountable is key to moving forward.

As a microbusiness owner, you will probably find that most of the time you are only accountable to yourself. You no longer have anyone breathing down your neck, checking what you have achieved every day, asking you for productivity reports, checking their watch when you leave at the end of the day, and appraising your performance on an annual basis. That's one of the best things about being self-employed.

You are now free to do as you will, set your own schedule, and take as long as you want to achieve what you want to achieve. Wonderful!

But, and it's a big but, you still need to be accountable to someone. If you're not, you may well find yourself getting to the end of the day, week, or even year, having achieved very little.

I am all too aware of how important a little accountability is to grow a microbusiness. If I'm going to be totally honest with you, I'm not great at keeping the promises I make to myself. For example, this book was on my 'things to do' list for over two years before I sat down and started making real progress on writing it. Two years! Two years of inactivity, procrastination and frustration that could have been spent so much more constructively. You could have had this book two years earlier if only I had been more accountable!

The key here is to understand what makes you accountable. If, like me, you struggle to be self-accountable, and find yourself continually letting yourself down because you just can't get motivated enough to do what you need to do, then you need to find another way. You need to figure out how to become motivated enough to potentially put yourself out of your comfort zone and do the difficult things.

It's important to understand that being accountable is not just about being responsible for getting something done, it's also, at the end of the day, about you being answerable for your actions. For microbusiness owners, this can be a real challenge. After all, who but you will know what you have achieved? It can be very easy to start deceiving yourself into thinking you're being more action focussed and accountable that you are being. Believe me, I have done more of this than I care to remember!

So, what did I do to become more accountable, and what can you do to overcome this challenge?

Firstly, it's important to fully understand why your goal matters. How will you feel when you achieve it? How will you feel if you don't? You might find it useful to refer to Chapter One at this stage and refresh yourself on the vision exercise you completed. Try to amplify the urgency of your vision, remember why you're in business, what you want to achieve and how you are going to feel once your vision becomes your reality. Really feel it! Once again, ask yourself, why does it matter?

Make a commitment

Once you're all fired up and ready to rock'n'roll it's time to make a commitment to yourself. How you do this will be different for everyone. I have listed a few ideas that have worked for me and that you might want to try:

Write it down and tick it off

I love doing this, it makes me feel like I have achieved so much. Even if some of the items on the list might be small it gives me a warm fuzzy feeling inside to tick them off. Setting deadlines for how many things you are going to tick off before you take a break can also work. It's about making a commitment to achieving something before moving on. I'll be talking more in the next chapter about finding the right productivity tool for you but for now, write it down and tick it off. Simple!

Get an accountability buddy or group of buddies

I would highly recommend this. Having someone, who isn't a family member, making you accountable can make a tangible difference. Knowing that someone else is going to have expectations of you, question you, and make you answerable for your own commitments can be a great motivator. I mentioned earlier that I spent two years thinking about writing this book and not actually writing it. Well, I eventually found myself an amazing author mentor who gave me the accountability I needed to start writing (thank you Gayle Johnson). Between us we planned the workload and set deadlines. I became accountable to her as well as to me – I overcame my inability to keep my promises to myself by making a promise to someone else instead.

Make public declarations

There's nothing quite like having the whole world watching what you are doing and waiting with bated breath on the outcome of your declaration. Be careful that people don't get fed up of you constantly making declarations for every little thing you need to achieve though. This is a good technique to use when you're setting yourself a big goal. Something that will encourage excitement in other people and keep them engaged with how you are progressing.

Keep taking action and moving forwards

If you are anything like me and the thousands of other microbusiness owners out there you will always have your eye firmly on maintaining high standards.

Now that must be a good thing, mustn't it? We all want to achieve great results for ourselves and for our clients, but what does doing a good job mean to you? Are you satisfied when you've given it your best – or must the fruits of your labour be nothing less than perfect?

High standards are essential in any business – but so is timing. By timing, I mean knowing when to complete one task and move on to the next. Understanding when the time is right to let your efforts loose onto the world, conclude your report or simply declare a job complete is key to getting things done. As well as having to work well, you also need to work efficiently, and stalling over details may cost you and your clients valuable time.

If you're stuck on a task – drafting and redrafting, trimming and refining, or, even worse, you've been incubating a killer idea for months but you've still to put pen to paper, you're suffering from perfection paralysis.

I am an excellent example of someone suffering from perfection paralysis. I used to go so far as to describe myself to people as a 'procrastinating perfectionist' – someone who would do a job very well tomorrow. Much of that was a result of fear. Fear of having to release my work into the big wide world; fear of being judged on the quality of my work; even fear of being successful perhaps.

In general, I'm a big picture person. But in business, I used to sweat the small stuff. A lot. I'm just not a 'that'll do' kind of person. I'm a 'that will certainly not do' kind of person. I don't just want my clients to be happy. I want them to be ecstatic with the work I produce for them. At the same time however I now understand the value of finishing a task and moving on. Perfection is not achievable so good enough is good enough!

If you are afraid your work won't be good enough, you're simply not going to let it go – but missed deadlines and a string of postponements are not taking you or your business anywhere. And worst of all – it doesn't work! Striving for improbable standards has also been proven to add to a string of health problems such as depression, eating disorders and relationship trouble – not the ideal conditions for successful business!

Moving your business forward requires agility, courage and the ability to launch your projects and ventures when the time is right – not when everything has been perfected.

The truth, painful as it is for perfectionists, is that you can't be perfect. It's impossible. Sorry. In fact, if you're doing something for the first time, which means you're taking a leap into the unknown, your best efforts might not be that great at all. How could they be, when you don't have any experience of what success might even look like? You need to embrace failure, or the 'not very good' attempts to get to the good stuff.

Here are my top tips for overcoming perfectionism:

Be Natural

Perfectionism is time-consuming – can your clients afford to wait? Can you afford to spend the time perfecting something when new projects, clients and products are calling for your attention?

Look at the natural world around you – even the pot plant on your desk – everything is in a permanent cycle of creation, growth, death and rebirth and crucially, nothing stays still. Life is characteristically a little messy and unpredictable. Nature never worries about perfection and neither should you.

Get Moving

It's time to break the block – and the only way to do this is to MOVE. Brainstorm, build something out of Lego, go for a run (ok, a brisk walk will do), ring a friend, anything to break the paralysis. Then try following these essential steps to be at your **BEST**.

As Mother Nature knows, it's all about **balance** – avoiding perfection paralysis as well as the other extreme of cutting corners to save time. Get to know when you're at your best and provide yourself with ideal conditions if you can – whether that's an early start and a working brunch, long afternoons at your desk or evenly-distributed blocks of work time punctuated with breaks.

Next you need some momentum – put some **energy** into the project. Focus your mind with meditation or breathing exercises – then... play! A playful attitude guarantees you'll be at your most relaxed and creative, so never forget to enjoy what you're doing.

Be **satisfied** with your efforts – glitches are OK. You will never stop improving so learn when to stop and let go.

At the same time, keep **trying**. If at first you don't succeed, try, try again. Then try again and try maybe one more time – then drop it and rest. Give yourself a pat on the back and a glass of wine – you did great!

Don't beat yourself up

True innovation means you give your projects your best shot and accept that until you release them into the wild (because that's how it feels sometimes!) and see how they fare, you're in the dark. And if the results are less than perfect, don't waste time beating yourself up. Just accept that you are where you're at, you're doing your best and you're learning all the time – which means you're now able to keep improving.

When you're running a microbusiness, you can't be an expert in everything, and you probably can't afford to hire experts to do everything either, so you're on a learning curve.

So, get on with that learning, and let go of the idea that you need to be great at everything the first time around. You can't afford to hold up your business progress by holding off until you think your projects are 'perfect'.

As I sit here writing I am doing some fast learning about how to put my thoughts down on paper, how to develop the marketing plan for my book, how to find a suitable publisher, that is, one that is willing to publish my book! I don't find it easy to feel that any of them are 'finished' until they have been perfected. However, as it's the first time I've really done any of these things, I'm not even sure what 'perfect' even is!

Bite Size Chunks

I am sure you will know the saying 'Rome wasn't built in a day'. Well think of your vision as Rome, and then think of every single little job that needs to be done to reach your vision as a single task. I mean, every single one! You'll never be able to do them all today so why even try?

It's so easy to set expectations of what we are going to achieve that are just ridiculous. I'm a big believer in breaking everything I do into small bite sized chunks. Every task might be tiny, but I get to the end of the day and I've achieved something tangible that makes me feel great!

Remember the list I talked about earlier? I love a list, and I love ticking things off my list even more than I love the list itself! Well, I'm going to tell you a secret… your list should only have things on it that you can achieve that day. It might only be two or three things, but every one of those things will actively move things forward.

How would having 'Build Rome' on your to-do list make you feel? Would you achieve it? I can confidently answer no to that question! But if your list was:

- Phone brick supplier to get costs of bricks
- Research the temperature of other Roman baths
- Order toga from the internet

How would that make you feel? Much better I'm sure, and you would end the day having achieved all three things.

It's such a great feeling when you can achieve what you set out to achieve, and it will also reduce your stress levels when you know that you have moved a project forward.

So, be kind to yourself, don't expect too much on a day by day basis, remove the stress by doing the little things, as eventually each little thing will grow into your vision.

Nurture yourself

It might not be instantly clear, but everything I've talked about so far in this chapter is about nurturing yourself. It's all about self-care. As microbusiness owners who work from home, we all need to take our self-care seriously, we need to look after ourselves. After all, who else is going to do it?

What you don't want is to find yourself sinking under the burden of what other people expect from you, clients, family and friends. I am also talking about the unrealistic expectations we have of ourselves. We need to free ourselves of this burden and allow ourselves to thrive in a positive, stress free environment.

It's clear to me, through experience, that:

- saying no to someone else means that you will be able to say yes to yourself
- having clearly communicated boundaries means that you can simply enforce them without any feelings of guilt
- slaying your 'What If Monster' will result in you being proud of how you can overcome your fears
- being accountable means that you are much more likely to achieve what you set out to achieve.
- setting realistic and achievable tasks will ensure you end the day on a high.

Can you remember in Chapter Two, I asked you the question, are you a good boss?

I talked about setting a good example for yourself and getting into habits that nurture rather than sabotage your business. I highlighted the importance of developing a structure and balance to your work day that reflects and enhances your own personal way of working, for example: Do you have regular breaks? Are you working with or against your body clock? And are you nurturing your body with exercise and healthy food?

Well, this chapter is also about how good a boss you are, but we have moved away from the practicalities of working from home and we have entered your less tangible inner world. It's about helping you to remove your personal inner barriers to getting things done. Ultimately your business growth depends on it.

This chapter has focussed on the habits and behaviours that enable us to be our best in business. Don't make the mistake of thinking this is a luxury or that it's self-indulgent – I'd go as far as to say without doing this work your business is doomed!

So rather than skim and read on, take some time to think about how these strategies are working for you right now, and what changes you might make to feel more in control. Then, using the bite-sized chunks approach I outlined earlier, give yourself three things to do each day to get you closer to this Thousandaire way of life. Your list will be deeply personal, as it depends on your personal challenges, but it might include something like:

- give myself time to think before saying yes when my client gets in touch
- take that big scary item from my to-do list and break it down into manageable chunks
- get an accountability buddy or join a group
- set clear working times for myself and let my family and clients

know what they are

- set contracts with clients which include when they can expect me to be available to them

Remember, as with anything to do with mindset, it's not a one-hit wonder! It's a bit like having a bath: you don't get clean once and think you're done for the rest of your life! The strategies that I outline in this chapter are ways of working that I return to again and again. I need to continually revisit them because, like most people, I don't get it right all the time. None of us will get it right all the time, like me, you'll have good days and bad days. Days that feel like you want to hide from the world and days when you feel positive, up-beat and optimistic about everything, however difficult you might sometimes find things. The trick is to develop habits and behaviours that anchor you through the thick and thin, so you don't give up on the bad days, and you don't burn out on the good ones!

As you continue reading the book, don't forget to keep working at the issues we've covered in this chapter. Use your Thousandaire journal to record your progress.

So, now we've addressed your inner self, it's time to start thinking about what's going on in the big wide world and how you can turn the Thousandaire model into reality for you.

Key Points

- Being a Thousandaire isn't just a business model – it's a mindset that lets you be your best

- It's OK to say no and set boundaries – it means you are saying yes to yourself and your business

- Think positive – replace the 'What If Monster' with a 'What if I fly?' mindset

- Get accountable to ensure you take action – accountability partners can help with this

- Break big projects down – create a manageable to do list and do it!

Chapter Six

GETTING READY:

The Practicalities

> "Organise, don't agonise."
> Nancy Pelosi

If I could show you a way to make your life as simple and uncomplicated as possible, would you want to know?

This chapter is about creating a business world that enables you to do things as smoothly as possible. It's about the practicalities of getting stuff done. It's about setting up systems. I love a good system, something that makes a task simpler, ensures deadlines are hit, and gives me confidence that everything is under control.

I don't think it matters what business you're in. Every business needs some sort of process or system to make sure that customer work is completed to deadline and that your internal business activities are controlled and achieved with as little stress as possible. Whether you run a virtual assistant business like mine which relies heavily on systems and processes to perform at our best for our clients, or a creative business that by its very nature is more focused on your inspiration, it doesn't matter, you still need processes and systems to stay on track.

So, what do I mean when I say 'process'? Well, a process is like a roadmap. It is a clear path that can be followed every time a task is done to ensure that you achieve a consistent result every time. A clearly documented process, or system, is one which can be shared and easily understood by anyone who needs to fill your shoes. In simple terms, it's an ABC of how to do something. All you need to do is follow the process and abracadabra the work will be completed without any stress and in superfast time. At least that's the theory!

Setting up processes is important for any business, but it's essential when you're moving from a complete DIY model to becoming a Thousandaire. When you're a Thousandaire you bring other people into the inner world of your business. They need to know how things work so they can do it too. Winging it with scraps of paper is likely to bring things to a crash, fast. So, before thinking about bringing in anyone else, work through this chapter to ensure your foundations are strong.

As usual, everything I talk about in this chapter is what has worked for me. It may or may not be exactly what you need in your business, but if one thing doesn't work for you, I guarantee that something else will. After all, every single one of us will have paperwork to process, tasks to complete, and deadlines to hit.

By the end of the chapter, you'll have a better understanding of:

- what a system or process is and how it can benefit you in your business
- how to organise your finances so you can still pay yourself at the end of the month
- how to get your paperwork and emails organised so they work for you
- productivity tools that help to effectively manage tasks and time
- how to start developing bespoke processes for your business

I feel like I want to make a declaration at this stage. I'm a control freak! There, I've said it! I'm in my happy place when I'm developing processes and benefiting from them. They truly keep me sane. I do understand however that not everyone is like me. What looks like chaos to me is perfectly clear and understandable to someone else. I remember, a long time ago, when I was working in the corporate world, being totally shocked to find someone sat at their desk behind a literal wall of paperwork. I'm not exaggerating when I tell you that it took some effort to see the person sat behind the desk! I couldn't even start to comprehend how that person could possibly work in that environment. My clear desk philosophy was really being tested. But I asked her a question and she dipped into the pile and immediately produced the bit of paper that provided the answer I needed. It was like a magic trick! Everyone's process is different.

If you like living behind a wall of paper, then just take what you can from this chapter and keep doing what works for you. If you want to streamline, there will be tools and tricks here to help you. The main point here is that however you work, whatever system you use, it's all fine if it makes life smoother rather than harder for you, your business and your growing team.

So, what are my 'must dos' for setting up as a Thousandaire?

- Organise your finances
- Organise your paperwork
- Use a task management system
- Manage your emails
- Organise your digital files
- Know your productivity tools

Let's take each of these in order.

Organise your finances

In my opinion there are three types of people in the world of microbusiness owners. Those who love playing about with their finances and having their finger on their financial pulse every minute of every day, those that will do pretty much anything else to avoid facing the fact that finances even exist and hope that the money will just happen somehow, and hybrids, people who love keeping on top of their financial records but find it hard to focus on the big financial picture. The latter is a beautiful example of me! I'm working on it though I promise!

It doesn't matter which one of the above you are right now, what matters is the robustness of your financial management systems as you grow your Thousandaire business. If you currently use an A4 accounts ledger, or if you use a carrier bag to store a year's worth of receipts before spending a week of your life entering them into your finance system, then you need to think again.

It's important as you enter this new model of working to ensure that your financial systems will support your business now and in the future. It's no longer appropriate to have haphazard financial systems that work for you but where nobody else has a clue what's going on.

Apart from ensuring that you have peace of mind and confidence in your financial systems, you will soon need, if you don't already, to consider how your systems impact on other people. Here are a few key questions that you might like to reflect on:

Could someone else take over your day to day finances, for example, raising your invoices, managing your credit control or being responsible for your bookkeeping? Ask yourself, is this possible right now? Could you outsource your finances with ease, or would it be a logistical nightmare?

Are you aware of your cash flow? Do you have confidence that you can pay your suppliers? As you grow your Thousandaire business you need to remember that your team members will want to be paid! And don't forget, so will you!

All these areas are key to running a successful Thousandaire business. You need to be able to outsource your finance at some point in the future, so why not get ready now? You need to pay your suppliers on time, or why would they work for you again? And you need to understand the costs involved in growing your team or you may end up financially out of pocket yourself.

Get yourself financially online

We are living and working in the 21st Century now and keeping a bag of receipts just doesn't make sense when you need to have your finger on your financial pulse. I recommend that you get set up with online banking and with online accountancy software. Having this will mean you can very easily keep your bookkeeping up to date and reconcile your accounts at the click of a button. My advice is to keep it online, keep it simple and spend just 5 minutes a day keeping on top of things. I promise you, you'll thank me later for this advice.

Get a good accountant

If you don't already use an accountant, then I would recommend that you find a great local accountant that can keep you on the right track with your annual accounts.

A good accountant is worth their weight in gold and should provide you with sound advice on everything you need to know financially, including advising you on what online software to use, providing you with some training and being on hand to answer any questions that you may have or to fix issues if you make a mistake. I've made quite a few myself so I have first-hand experience of how useful a good accountant can be.

I would recommend checking that the price you pay includes being available to ask questions and sort out simple problems. What you don't want is an accountant who charges you by the minute for every phone call and query – the cost will soon stack up and you'll end up with an unexpected bill at the end of the month. Nightmare!

Get your paperwork organised

Do you ever run around the house looking for a specific bit of paper that you need for something, like theatre tickets, a bill you need to pay today or perhaps you need to find the directions you printed off for that meeting you're going to in 30 seconds time? Where did you leave it? Was it on the kitchen table? Was it with the other pile by the front door? Is it in your bag? Who knows? Aaaaggghhh!

Don't worry if that rings true for you, you can start to relax and breath more easily once you start using the following system.

It really couldn't be any simpler, and it's a system that I first used many years ago when I was working as a PA to a CEO. His office and his diary were an administrative nightmare and as busy as anything you can imagine, and this system kept me sane and kept him organised, and I have been using it ever since.

It's about having a place for everything and having everything in its place, and it's all based around four folders. Quite simply, every single piece of paper that crosses your desk should be systematically and consistently put into one of those four folders. Simple, yes?

So, what do you need to do? To get started you need to invest in your four folders. I would recommend getting the following:

- Three A4 document wallets
- One concertina folder with the months and dates along the top

Then label them as follows:

- Action
- Pending
- Bring Forward (this is the concertina folder)
- Filing & Scanning

Action

This is for the paper that you need to action straight away. It's for work that is current and requires your attention today. Any paper, scribbled notes and everything else that relates to the work you are going to be doing today needs to go in this file.

It is basically a reflection of your to-do list that day.

I also use my inbox as my electronic action folder. I will be talking a bit later in this chapter about using your inbox strategically.

Pending

Everything in this folder is for paper that you can't progress because you are waiting for someone else to action something. If you're waiting to hear back from your web designer for example about the images you want adding to your website all paperwork relating to this should be in this folder.

I don't agree with printing everything off just so I can pop it in my pending folder, so my sent emails folder works in parallel to my pending file. I will be talking about this in more detail later in the chapter.

The purpose of having a pending folder is as a memory jogger. If you're busy running your business and juggling work priorities it can be easy to forget something, and the pending folder acts as your memory. You can very quickly flick through it every day and then you can forget all about it until the next day when you flick through again.

It's a good idea to pop a note at the top right-hand side of the paperwork when you have chased things up. For example, if you phoned and chased on Tuesday, write the date and a brief note about the discussion and agreed actions. This is a great way to keep on top of things rather than just relying on the other person to do their bit, and you won't have to remember every conversation you have, it'll all be there in black and white for you (or whatever colour pen you use) to easily refer to at a later date.

As soon as you have received a response you can move it into your action or filing folder. Simple!

Bring Forward Folder (the concertina file)

A bring forward folder is a paper reflection of your calendar and planned task list. Any paperwork related to any calendar appointment or pre-planned task is neatly filed away in the appropriate date. So, how does it work?

I use a concertina folder with the month and days of the month clearly labelled at the top of each section. January to December and 1 to 31. You could use a ring binder with clearly labelled pockets, or a drawer with labelled folders. It doesn't really matter what stationery you use, it's the system that matters.

Any papers that you have for the future should be filed here. I thought it would be helpful to give you a few examples of the sort of things you may want to use the bring forward folder for:

Train tickets for a journey two months from now – these should be filed horizontally in the month you are travelling (so you don't have to look at them). When that month comes around sort through all that month's paperwork and then file everything upright in the relevant date. Then when the day comes all you need to do is pick them up and go!

Papers for a meeting that you are attending later in the month – these should be filed upright in the relevant date. Put on your coat, grab your bag and pick up your papers and you're off! No more scrabbling around trying to find what you need with 30 seconds to go.

Paperwork related to a project that you want to work on next week

– these should be filed upright in the relevant date that reflects your planned task list.

Basically, everything you need for a future meeting or task should either be filed in the relevant month for anything beyond the current month, or in the relevant date for anything in the current month. Once a new month begins you can sort through everything for that month and pop it in the appropriate date.

It might take you a short while to get to grips with using this system but once you get into the flow of it you will never look back. I promise you that!

Filing and Scanning

Anything that has been completed and needs either filing or scanning electronically can go in this folder. When you have five minutes spare one day you can get it all filed. I tend to scan anything I need to keep. It takes up less space, and in my opinion, it is far easier to find when I need it.

Like I mentioned earlier, this system is about having a place for everything and having everything in its place. This is important for any business, and if it's just you in your business then using this system will keep you organised and in control. Brilliant! But if you're following the Thousandaire growth model and planning on bringing other people into your business it becomes critical.

Once you have a team working in your business it won't just be you who needs to find the paperwork related to an ongoing project for example, so it can't just be in your head, it can't just be your system, it must be the business's system.

Don't let your tasks manage you!

It's important to keep on top of your task list and having a system to help you do this will not only save you time and make your life easier, it will actively ensure that deadlines are met, client expectations are exceeded, and best of all, you remain calm throughout.

Finding the right tool for you is important. Do you need it just for you? Do you work within a team that need to be able to share and contribute?

It's not about what system you use, it's about having a task management system that works for you. You might like to keep a paper task list, or perhaps you already use the task function in Outlook or similar. If it's working for you then I suggest you keep using it but it's important that it keeps you on track, tells you when a task is due and allows you to allocate tasks to other people when necessary.

Personally, I prefer to use an online task management tool. There are lots of them available all of which are great, but the one I use, and which works well for me, my team and our clients, is Trello (www.trello.com). It can be used effectively for small one-off tasks, repeat tasks and larger projects, and to be honest I don't know where my business would be without it!

Like all good systems though it needs to be used effectively, whether it's just you in your business currently or you have already started to grow your team, it doesn't matter. A system can only be as useful and effective as the information being put in to it, and the people using it.

If it's worth having a system in the first place it's worth making sure it's kept up to date and current. There's absolutely no point having a system that just sits there, it needs to be an integral part of your business, and it needs to do what you want it to do.

Get on top of your emails

Just the thought of having a long list of emails in my inbox makes me shiver with dread! I really am a control freak and having too many emails in my inbox can leave me feeling unsettled and out of control, so I have a tried and tested system for keeping my inbox clear and my mind settled.

So, how do I do that? Firstly, I have a robust filing system for my emails. Every client, team member, supplier etc. has their own folder, and once an email has been actioned it either gets filed away or deleted.

Remember in Chapter Four I talked about using the 4Ds method for prioritising your activities? Well, I use this method effectively with my emails. I usually only look at an email once before I decide which of the 4Ds I allocate it to as follows:

DO IT

I action it immediately because it's <u>urgent and important</u>. Then I file it away. If I need a response to an email, I keep it safely in my Sent Items. This acts as my electronic pending folder as I mentioned above.

DATE IT

I put it in my task list or in my diary for a future date because it's <u>important but not urgent</u>. I attach the email itself, so I can then file or delete the original email.

DELEGATE IT

I forward it to a team member to action because it's <u>urgent but not important</u>. Once again, I keep the sent email safely in Sent Items until I receive a response. This acts as a memory jogger. Alternatively, it could be put into your task management system (as above).

DUMP IT

This speaks for itself, I think. If it's <u>not urgent and not important</u> why do you need it? Delete it!

As I mentioned above, all sent emails are either deleted, filed or left in my Sent Items until I receive a reply. My Sent Items work in parallel to my pending folder (see above). It's my memory jogger for items that I am still awaiting a response from.

Your online filing cabinet

Filing used to be an exercise in opening and closing filing cabinet drawers and putting things in alphabetical order. It's evolved over time to be predominantly an exercise in dragging and dropping electronic files, although you do still need to know your alphabet. Whatever the changes, the essence of filing is still the same. It's a mundane but essential business activity that ideally should be done on a regular basis to ensure that you keep on top of things. I talked earlier about having a folder for filing and scanning as part of the 'get your paperwork organised' section. But where should you file everything?

As usual, I'm all about keeping things simple, and setting up a robust and easily understood filing system is part and parcel of running a microbusiness. You may still be filing your paperwork in a big gloomy looking filing cabinet, but to be honest, as home workers, who really wants one of those in the corner of their home? I certainly don't!

I recommend finding a good online file storage system. There are loads around and you may already have access to one if you use Office 365 or have an Apple account. The one I currently use very successfully is called Dropbox (www.dropbox.com). You simply set up your filing system, for example, your top-level folder might be called Admin, and then sub folders may be Finance, Recruitment, Marketing etc, and further sub folders under finance might be something like Invoices, Credit Control, Annual Rate Increases etc.

Some points to consider:

- Does it need to be a shared system?
- Use obvious names for your folders so you can find your way round easily – go with how your brain works
- Do you have a dating system within your files? If a folder has multiple files then I find it helpful to name the files by the date, for example 20190324mybook (this format allows you to sort in a date sequence).
- Do you have an archive file?

Backing up

This is critical to your peace of mind. It's about disaster recovery. This might sound a bit dramatic but consider what would happen if you lost your files – now I'm sure that would be a disaster for you, yes?

We file everything online using Dropbox, and this is automatically backed up on our behalf. But what would happen if the internet disappeared overnight? Maybe I'm being overly cautious, but I also back up onto a hard drive to be certain that nothing is lost in the event of a disaster.

Taking some time to consider this now might save you a lot of trouble and effort in the future. So, I encourage you to consider your options for backing up your files. What do you currently do? What would happen if your laptop was lost or stolen? How would you recover your files?

Productivity Systems

Have you ever got to the end of a working day and wondered where all your time had gone? I can honestly say that much of my working life has been spent jumping from task to task, trying to juggle numerous jobs all at the same time, and being proud of what a great multi-tasker I was. The problem was, I was doing lots of things but not necessarily in the most productive way.

So, how can you manage your time so that your day is as productive as possible?

My lightbulb moment came during an event I went to during my first year in business. The person running the event asked for a show of hands from everyone who had a time management problem. The response was unanimous. Arms and hands were waving wildly around as people willingly admitted their time management shortcomings. His response to this enthusiastic response was to ask us whether we ever go on holiday. Do we get to the airport on time, catch our plane, and take a holiday for two weeks? If we do, then we don't have a time management problem at all – we have a problem with prioritisation.

I thought this was fascinating. We can all manage ourselves perfectly well when we need to. The problem comes when we don't give enough time to the things we are supposed to be doing, and we spend too much time on the things we're not supposed to be doing.

Allocating time to our tasks is a huge part of how we manage our day. When we're multi-tasking, we're allocating tiny slots of time to different tasks and switching repeatedly – real multi-tasking is scientifically impossible! We can only focus on one thing at a time.

I do however think that multi-tasking can be a positive activity, enabling you to move very quickly from one essential task to the other. But what about when you really need to focus?

I have a few tried and tested ways to get back into the swing of things as follows:

Break it down

In Chapter Four I talked about using the 4Ds model as a straightforward and simple way to prioritise what needs to be done on any specific day. It's a great system and it works well, most of the time. There are however some days when it works less well and, to be honest, those days are usually when I'm just not feeling it, when I'm tired, feeling a bit 'bleugh', and everything feels a little bit too hard.

Sometimes when I'm feeling like this I listen to my inner needs and allow myself some time to rest and nurture myself before cracking on with what I need to do. But sometimes the work is too important to ignore, and I need to find a way to overcome my lack of motivation. So, what do I do?

I had an amazing revelation a few years ago when I stumbled across a fantastic time management tool – a giant sand timer. It's 24cm high, has bright green sand, and it takes exactly half an hour to run through. I love it!

It's ideal for those times when you just need to get on with something. I turn off my phone, close Outlook and work on a single task for half an hour.

There are some tasks in business that we resist and put off for days, weeks or months, because we don't know where to start, or we think and believe it will be a very unpleasant experience.

But once you sit down and tackle it, it's quite enjoyable – and you'll feel brilliant when you've finished. However bad it is, half an hour is manageable. If the task feels impossible, a good tactic is to devote one of your half-hour slots to simply looking at it, breaking it down and gathering the information or paperwork you need to make a start.

Eventually, sand timing your work gets to be good fun. You get to the point where, when the sands are running thin, you focus even more strongly and race it. When the sands are all gone, you can stop and do something else. However, often, you'll turn it over and do another half hour.

You don't need a real-life sand timer to benefit from this method. There are plenty of 'pomodoro' technique (a time management method developed by Francesco Cirillo in the late 1980s) apps or websites that work on the same principle. These apps allow you to set a timer for a chunk of time (usually 25 minutes) then take a short break – turning a mammoth task into something more manageable.

Use the 'I'll just...' method

This is another great and simple way to get started on something when you're feeling a bit stuck. Particularly if it's a bit of a project and it all feels a little overwhelming.

Just say to yourself 'I'll just...'. For example, 'I'll just read the first chapter...', or 'I'll just sort out the paperwork ready to start work...'. You're basically tricking your mind into believing that all you're going to do is the smallest task that will just get you started on a project, but once you get started you might just surprise yourself and keep going. You might also just do what you set out to do, and that's ok too. At least you'll have done something, you'll have progressed in some small way, and like I keep saying, every step, however small, moves you toward your final goal.

Track your time

Do you sometimes get to the end of your day and feel like you've been busy but unproductive? Do you feel like you spend half your life running around and not achieving anything? Being busy used to be a sign of productivity for me, a sign that I had worked hard. Yes, I was working hard, but I had it all topsy-turvy about the productivity part of the equation. The reality was that I was probably wasting as much time as I was spending on productive work.

All the work we do for clients is focused and logged in a systematic and effective way. So, I asked myself 'why don't I do this for everything I do over a working day?', and I decided to give it a try and see what the results were.

I logged my time over a month. Everything I did was logged. Making a cup of tea, spending time on social media, shuffling bits of paper around my desk, walking the dog, hanging out the washing, everything! The results were fascinating. Some of those activities are necessary parts of my day (walking the dog, for example) but there were a few things that I needed to change to make my day as productive as possible - for example the amount of time I spent on social media (and I bet I'm not the only one!).

There are several time logging tools available but the one I use is called Toggl (www.toggl.com). It's simple and if used well will be a good friend to you and your business.

Be prepared for night time musings

Do you keep a pad and pen by your bed? If not, why not? You may be able to sleep like a baby most of the time, or maybe you're someone who roams the night drinking camomile tea and banging your head against the wall in frustration because you just can't drop off. Either way, if you have a pad and pen by the side of your bed, you can jot down any night time thoughts and ideas that might be keeping you awake.

I have lots of great ideas in the middle of the night and in the past, I'd be patting myself on the back congratulating myself on my creativity and ingenuity before dropping off to sleep, only to wake up the next day having completely forgotten it all. I did this for years before quite literally waking up to the fact that all I needed to do was write it down.

It's a very simple yet very effective way to off-load any night time musings, good and bad. If you're feeling stressed, you can jot down a few actions that you need to take in the morning to sort out the problem; if you are inspired and excited, putting it down in words will allow you to sleep soundly knowing that in the morning you won't even have to try to remember. It works both ways and I highly recommend giving it a go, I promise you, both your sleep and your business will benefit!

My first thoughts about this book were in a dream. I woke up with a clear idea about the book title and the concept. I got out of bed and wrote it all down and as a result I slept like a baby and didn't have to try to remember it all the next day.

Develop your own processes

Most of the systems, processes and tools that I talk about above are universally useful. Your business however is unique, and although I recommend that you consider using some or all the above methods, you may also want to consider developing your own bespoke processes or merging some of the systems to create a hybrid. It doesn't matter what process you end up using, what matters is that it works for you and for your business. Remember that other people will soon be in your business, so keep things as clear and simple as possible.

Here are some prompts for creating your own systems successfully:

Map out your current activities

Take some time to assess all the key tasks in your business. Jot down anything you do on a regular basis, whether daily, weekly, monthly or annually.

Then ask yourself:

- What processes and systems do I currently use? Write this down step by step.
- How do they work?
- How could things be improved?
- What gaps are there?
- Which tasks would benefit most from being systemised?

I think it's a good idea at this stage to list the tasks in order of priority to ensure the most critical are dealt with first. These may be the tasks that would increase turnover or improve customer service, things that can have a fast and direct impact on your customers.

Know what your ideal outcome would be

Once you have identified the first task to be systemised think about what your ideal outcome is. What does the perfectly finished task look like?

Then start working backwards with each step being clearly identified from the final perfect outcome right back to the start of the task. I recommend writing these down as you go. What also works well is to get creative with coloured pens and flip chart paper and keep adding stages until you have covered every single step of the way. It really doesn't matter how you do it, number them, colour code them, do whatever you need to do to get every step of your task down on paper, then put them in the order they need to be completed.

You can then compare what you have now to what you currently do. Keep an eye open for any steps that are duplicated or unnecessary. It needs to be as simple as ABC, like I mentioned earlier in the chapter, and it needs to be easily understood and implemented by someone else. Remember, it's not your system, it's the business's system.

It's no longer just about you - this is key to creating a strong Thousandaire model.

Add logical breaks

Depending on the complexity of the task you might want to consider adding logical breaks. What do I mean by that? Well, raising monthly invoices to clients for example, may have a few key logical breaks. Firstly, drafting, then checking and authorising, and finally raising and issuing the invoices. Even if you are the only person in your business completing this task, there are still three distinctly logical breaks to the task. It might be that one part requires a template or check list, another a form for signature, and the final step may benefit from a more staged process which leads seamlessly to the credit control task.

Test and adjust

This is self-explanatory. Test your system in the real world, consider how things go as you progress, and make any necessary revisions, and if you can, simplify it even further.

Now, I want to be clear that you really don't need to over complicate anything when it comes to processes. The point is that you need to have a process that anyone can follow, that saves time, and that ultimately provides you with a strong platform on which your business can grow. Please, please don't create a new process if you genuinely think that it's not going to do any of this.

This point also leads neatly on to my next recommendation:

If you don't use it, lose it!

You'll know by now that I love a good system! But however much I believe in the power of systems and tools to keep me on track, I also think that sometimes they can act purely as a barrier rather than as an enabler to productivity. It's always worthwhile when thinking about introducing new processes and systems, to take a good look at everything in your business and see what you currently do that just doesn't help. What can you get rid of? What processes have you already got that just give you a job to do but don't actively add value?

I remember, when I was at school, I would spend absolutely ages planning my revision. I would create the most beautiful revision timetable, all coloured in, with blocks of time planned in for each subject. It really was a work of art. But it didn't enable me to get my revision done. In fact, it did the opposite. Once I had finished creating my masterpiece, it was out of date and needed to be done again. It was an active barrier to my revision, and I should have binned it and just opened my books. If I had used my sand timer method or my 'I'll just…' method I would have got a lot more done with a lot less drama.

In other words, clear the decks for systems, processes and tools that make your life easier rather than harder. Consider what you've currently got but don't use. Why don't you use them? Are they potentially useful or do they just pile on the guilt because you're not using them? Are they, like my revision timetable was for me, keeping you busy but unproductive?

In simple terms, if you don't use it, lose it!

This chapter has focussed on the systems and tools that enable your business to run as smoothly and seamlessly as possible. After all, a business, however small, will always benefit from being systemised and organised, and making sure the systems you adopt are future proofed will not only keep you on track right now, they will also provide you with a robust platform for growth. The key to running an effective system or process is to keep it up to date. Don't let it get out of hand. What will take you five minutes today, will undoubtedly turn into a nightmare task if you leave it unattended. Running a microbusiness with good systems and tools to hand that enable you to work through the tough times will not only help you sleep at night, they will actively run you and your business for you.

Key Points

- Map your current systems – what are they and how are they working for you?

- Your systems belong to your business, not you. What do you do automatically or intuitively that needs systematising or explaining so others can do it too?

- Get your finances online, and invest in a good accountant

- All paperwork, online files and emails should be easy to find – use the 4Ds model to help you organise

- Keep things simple – break things down into half hour or 'I'll just…' blocks

- What systems can you lose? Remember, if you don't use it, lose it!

Chapter Seven
MAKING IT HAPPEN

> "We are not a team because we work together.
> We are a team because we respect,
> trust and care for each other."
> Vala Afshar

I can't believe how far we've come together, and how much you have already achieved. So far, you've spent a lot of time reflecting and preparing for business growth and it's at this point that you can really start to get going. Fantastic! Not only do you already have the Thousandaire mindset, but you'll soon be able to put everything in this book into action – if you haven't already started that is!

This chapter is all about making it happen. It's about the practicalities of building a team around you and getting to grips with your new role in your business as a leader instead of a doer.

I should reiterate that what I am sharing with you here is what has worked for me. It really isn't a one size fits all solution, but if you're new to running a microbusiness, and if you have the Thousandaire mindset and would like to grow your business, then this is a great place to start.

As I talked about in Chapter Four, The Thousandaire model is about finding trusted associates who can replicate what you do and allow you to increase your client base beyond your own personal capacity. With that in mind, I want to be clear that everything I talk about in this chapter is:

- about recruiting associates rather than employees. Employment brings with it a myriad of HR responsibilities and red tape that outsourcing to associates does not. So, if you are planning to recruit an employee, do read on, as there's still lots of great stuff that you can use, but also consult with a HR professional to make sure you're doing everything right and in accordance with the law.

- from the perspective of my virtual assistant business. If you're making widgets then it might not matter to your client *who* is making the widget, what matters is the consistency in quality and customer service that they receive. If, however, like me, you provide a service that relies heavily upon having a great one-to-one relationship with your clients, it's far more complex getting the right match.

Whatever your business, I recommend you read through the chapter then apply it to your business as you feel appropriate.

At this stage I encourage you to refer to your Thousandaire journal to remind yourself of your vision, your values, and everything you've learned so far about your business and you in your business. It's all going to be useful to you as you progress through this chapter.

By the end of the chapter, you'll have a better understanding of:

- how to keep your clients happy as you grow your team
- how to recruit and build your team
- how to change your role from a business doer to a business leader

Ensuring your clients are happy

Wouldn't it be amazing if we could set up our microbusiness with a team of associates ready to start working for us on day one? You could focus all your time on finding your first client and then pass the work immediately to a team member. Brilliant! To be honest with you, I think that could be the perfect example of being a Thousandaire!

In the real world however, this is very unlikely to happen. All the microbusiness owners I know have initially taken on work themselves before even starting to consider their business growth strategy. The main reason for this is that, like most of us, they need every penny they can earn in the first few years of being in business.

As a result, when the time comes to recruit an associate and to start delegating your client work you must make a crucial decision:

- Do you transfer all your current clients over to someone else?
- Or, do you keep them yourself and find new clients for your associates to work with?
- Or, do you plan a hybrid approach by transferring some work but not all?

The choice is very much up to you, and everyone will do it slightly differently to suit their own personal circumstances. Your guiding thought will be about ensuring there is continuity in the quality of service for your clients. I chose to move from being the sole deliverer in my business to delegating all client work to my team.

How I did it

One of the trickiest things I had to do before I could start to delegate was to introduce the idea of outsourcing to my current clients. Many of my clients had been working with me personally for many years and we had built a strong trusting relationship, so why would they want to change?

How were my clients going to respond? What would they think? Would I lose them? What if it all goes wrong?

These were just a few of the concerns that I had. In all honesty, it took me two years to fully hand over all my direct client work. It was a slow process but one that I was fully committed to.

So, how did I do it?

I am a big believer in being as honest and transparent with my clients as I can possibly be, and this meant being up front about my plans to grow my business and to start introducing other team members into the mix. It was a good news story after all: I wasn't abandoning my clients, I was offering them a service that enhanced what I already did. I was adding value by:

- providing a seamless service that was robust enough to deal with high work levels, holidays and sickness. They now had two PAs for the price of one! How could they argue with that?
- providing additional skills that my new associate had that I didn't. Again, who wouldn't want that?

Good communication was a key factor in how I moved things forward. I was upfront about my motivation for growing the business, I reassured them that they would only ever work with someone that they could talk to and approve in advance. I even involved them in the recruitment process on one occasion.

The better our communication and the more involved my clients were in the whole process the smoother the transition became. I also regularly asked for feedback and responded to any hints of dissatisfaction. I've learned over many years that client complaints can usually be transformed into great customer satisfaction if you actively listen to the complaint, reassure them that you will act, and ultimately solve the problem for them. It's about making your clients feel loved and cared for.

Your clients need to know that you are delegating the work but you're not delegating the responsibility. It's your business, they're your clients and at the end of the day you will always be responsible for the work produced, whoever does it.

At first, it was a slow and gradual release of client work to my very first associate. I started off by using my associate to cover for when I was on holiday or poorly, for specific non-client facing pieces of work, or for those times when my workload was just too much for me to handle by myself.

Over time, my associate proved to me how brilliant she was, how much I could rely on her to do what she said she was going to do, how much I could trust her, and most importantly of all, she slowly built a great trusting relationship with my clients too.

This gradual process of delegating more and more work meant that when I wanted to hand over the work in its entirety the client was happy and settled with my associate already.

Remember the financial tipping point I talked about in Chapter Four? Gradually handing over client work to your associate will mitigate the financial dip that paying associates will inevitably result in. It means you keep most of your current income and start to slowly increase your income from associate work as your client base grows.

Whatever strategy you choose there is one critical thing you need to do right now - recruit your replacement. Firstly, remember that nobody can fully replace you, you are special, you really are, and don't you forget it!

Building your team around you

Congratulations! You have your vision, you understand your values and you are at this stage considering recruiting your first team member. You really are a Thousandaire! Your business will soon have the capacity for growth beyond your personal skills and how many hours you can work each day.

Do you remember the imaginary time machine that I talked about in Chapter Four? I explained how you could work for a client all day and then go back and do it all over again for another client, then again, and again, until your productivity and earning potential reached your wildest dreams. Or you could build a team around you that would effectively do the same thing with a lot less effort from you, and with a lot less of the travelling backwards and forwards in time. Well, this is how I did it...

Employee or Associate

Now, you have two choices at this stage, you can employ someone, or you can outsource work to an Associate. Employing staff for a microbusiness owner can be expensive and riddled with problems. In my experience outsourcing to highly trained and experienced associates has always worked well. But you must choose wisely.

Here are the key differences between an employee and an associate:

- An associate is self-employed. They should be an expert in their field, and they will probably be actively marketing their services to other people. They might not be working just for you and your clients.
- An associate is responsible for their own tax and National Insurance.
- An associate will invoice you for work completed. They are not on your payroll.
- You don't have to pay for holiday or sick leave. Your associate will be responsible for this themselves.

Remember that making a mistake with your recruitment, employed or otherwise, can have a devastating and far reaching effect on your business. After all, as a microbusiness owner, it is your reputation at stake. The buck will most definitely stop with you! Don't be scared off by this though. Risk is always part of business growth and if you understand the risks involved, and mitigate them successfully, the results will be fabulous. And when you get it right you will reap all the rewards too.

With your reputation at stake, your business growth reliant on finding the right people, and your future as a Thousandaire on the line, you really don't want to get it wrong. I was lucky as being a PA brings with it some real benefits, and in this instance, it is the love of producing systems and processes for any work that needs to be done more than once. As soon as I decided to grow my team, I immediately knew that having a robust recruitment system would help. Not only with my immediate recruitment needs but for all my team growth needs in the future. Why do something ten times when you only need to do it once and then copy?

There are a few things I always consider when recruiting team members to outsource work to and they are:

Clarity on the type of person and the role

Are you clear on the type of personality you need in your business?

It's not always the best idea to recruit a 'mini me' – in other words someone really like you. If you want to be challenged or if you want someone to bring a new perspective to your business, then perhaps you need to take on someone who is different to you. That said, however, if your new team member is going to be doing the same job as you, with the same clients, and with the same tools, then perhaps a 'mini me' is just what you need.

My main point is that you really need to consider the role you are recruiting for, what skills the applicants need, and what personal characteristics you want them to have in order to successfully fulfil the role. You don't want a big picture person if you need detailed work completing, and you may not want someone who focusses on statistics and details if you need them to lead the team. In simple terms, if you don't have total clarity on the person you want and the skills they need, how are you going to know when you find the right person? Will you be relying purely on gut feeling?

In addition to this, but of equal importance, you should always focus on your values, as highlighted in Chapter One. Having the right skills, for example, the ability to organise, plan and prioritise tasks; and the right personal characteristics, for example, being approachable and cooperative; are critical, but without your core values being aligned it will never work. Microbusinesses are exactly that - small but perfectly formed! Having a team member that doesn't have similar values to you will not work.

At the end of the day, it's your business, and you are the only person who has a full insight into who you need to develop it. One final piece of advice at this stage would be to trust your instincts. I am a stickler for job descriptions and person specifications but at the end of the day, however good the applicant appears, I always listen to what my gut is telling me. If I 'feel' that something is not quite right, then I listen and act accordingly. If I 'feel' that there is a real opportunity with someone who may not be a 100% fit, then I also take that into consideration when making my decision.

I have shared with you (see appendix) the person specification and job description that I developed for new PA team members within my own business. You may find this useful as an example and feel free to utilise as much or as little of it within your own business if it helps, but make sure you develop your recruitment system in line with your own specific needs.

Knowing where to advertise

So, you have your job description and person specification, and you know what values you are looking for in your new team member, but how are you going to find suitable applicants? This really is the million-dollar question!

In my experience it's either feast or famine when it comes to applications to join my team. Sometimes I get hundreds of applications, sometimes just a few, so knowing where to advertise is crucial if you want consistency and most importantly quality of applications. Where you advertise will be very industry specific but here are just a few ideas that you might want to consider:

- Social Media – Facebook, Twitter, LinkedIn etc. Communicating across channels and sharing on relevant groups.
- Recruitment sites – Indeed, Total Jobs etc. There are lots of these sites around so I would recommend doing a bit of research first and finding out the costs. Some let you advertise for free initially.
- Your website.
- Referrals from current team members – do they know anyone they could introduce?

Hopefully you will receive lots of great applications but how are you going to know when you have found the ideal person? There is no 100% fool proof way of ensuring you don't make the wrong choice, but you can mitigate the risk further by testing your applicant's skills, values and ability to work well within your business. My mantra is 'test, test, and then test again'!

So, what do I mean by this? Well, I believe in making it hard for anyone to join my team.

Application form

I test an applicant's motivation by insisting that they complete an application form. Having to complete a detailed application form is far harder than sending out a standard curriculum vitae. It requires time and effort and will test how much they want to become part of your team.

The application form needs to be faultless: no typos and well formatted. All communication from this stage onwards, whether it be in person, via email or telephone is tested for quality. Every contact with your applicant is an opportunity to test them. Use it!

Initial screening calls

If I'm interested in an application then I make an initial unplanned call to the applicant. This is simply a sifting exercise and gives me the opportunity to find out the following:

- What is their telephone manner like?
- Are they aware that the role is part time?
- Are they aware that this is a self-employed role?
- Are they happy with the rate of pay?
- What is my 'gut feeling' about the applicant?

Interviews

In my opinion, you can't fully understand what makes a person tick until you get eye to eye contact with them. How are their interpersonal skills? Do they answer your questions fully or are they evasive? I have sometimes held interviews in person and at other times used video conferencing. I don't think it matters that much if you can see each other and get eye contact. I recently held an online interview where the applicant was very obviously sat on their bed – this wasn't a great start and you won't be surprised to know that they didn't join my team.

Take time to consider what questions you are going to ask before the interview. Test what they have said on their application forms. Encourage a deeper discussion about things that are unclear or lacking detail. In other words, get them to prove to you that they are who you are looking for.

Skills testing

Application forms and interviews are all well and good but at the end of the day you need to know for certain that they have the skills you need. The only true way of knowing this is to test them.

Develop a few skills-based tests as part of the application process. If you need your recruit to build widgets, then get them to build a widget. It sounds simple because it is simple, but if you want them to hit the ground running you need to put them to the test.

I also find it useful at this stage to provide the candidate with a little constructive negative feedback. Even if they have done a fabulous job, I test how they respond. You really don't need a team member, however perfect they are for the job, if they react badly to feedback that is intended to help them learn and develop. This also leads neatly into the next area:

Attitude testing

I always question and test throughout the whole process what I call the applicants 'give a damn attitude'. Not necessarily a value but it does give me an insight into what makes them tick and answers lots of questions for me that I think should be inherent in anyone in any business, for example:

- Do they care about the quality of their work?
- Do they care about your client and their businesses?
- Do they care if they make a mistake?

Psychometric tests

You may also want to consider utilising psychometric testing during your recruitment process. This can be costly but if done well the information you gain will be invaluable and it will help you to make a final decision if you are nervous about taking the plunge, or if you are torn between two applicants. It may be the deal breaker.

I remember the first time I recruited using psychometric testing. I had the choice of two amazing candidates. They both scored extremely well on their application, their interview, and the work testing. I just couldn't choose between them. So, I asked them both to complete a psychometric test. The results were clear. One person was perfect for the job, the other would prove to be difficult to manage. What did I do? I took on the candidate who was perfect for the job of course. But that's not the end of the story... A few months later I was desperate for another team member, nobody was applying for the role and in my desperation I contacted the other applicant and offered her the job. It didn't take me long to realise what a mistake I'd made. Not only was she difficult for me to manage, she was also difficult with my clients! To cut a very long story short, she didn't last long.

References

Always, and I mean always, take up references. Even though you are a microbusiness, indeed because you are a microbusiness, you need to prove to yourself in as many ways as possible that your new associate is the right person for you. What better way than to find out about your new team member from someone they have worked with directly before.

Contracts

This is very important. I would recommend that you never outsource work to an associate without first having a contract in place. Now, this might sound like I don't trust my associates. That really isn't the case but having a contract in place provides my associates with clear parameters on what I expect from them and what they can expect from me. It clearly lays out:

- the scope of the work they will be doing
- the payment terms
- the intellectual property rights
- confidentiality and data protection responsibilities
- the obligations of both parties
- terms of termination
- the rules of sub-contracting
- clear guidance on the non-solicitation of clients
- and other areas that need to be clear before any working relationship can move forward.

I would highly recommend talking to a contract solicitor before handing over your client work to anyone else. It might be a significant upfront expense, but it will stand you in good stead if you have any problems in the future.

Of course, none of us will get it right all the time. I am sure, like me, you will make mistakes along the way, but if you spend the time considering all the above points, creating a system to help you focus on what matters, and listening to your gut then I am sure you will get it right most of the time.

Having said all of that, my first team member came along purely by chance! I was contacted by someone wanting to start working in the same field as me. We went for a coffee in the local garden centre, really liked each other, and pretty much started working together the next day. Ten years on and we are still working together, she has become an integral part of my business, and I would be devastated if she ever left me. So, although my recommendation of really understanding who you need in your business and what they bring to the table is true, sometimes you just need to be in the right place at the right time and fate will play its part.

Managing expectations

One of the trickiest things I have had to learn to manage is how to balance the short-term expectation of my associates with what I can offer them. What do I mean by this? Well, you want more clients, so you need to grow your team, but you really need your new team members before you get your new clients otherwise you risk letting your clients down – obviously this is not acceptable, but you might end up with a lovely new team member with nothing to do. So, how do you overcome this Catch 22 situation?

Don't over commit

Make sure each new team member you bring on board is fully aware that the work might start slowly but grow as you find new clients for them to work with. On a positive note, this gives them time to familiarise themselves with your business, get to know the rest of the team, and start to help with work that isn't client facing.

Find new clients

Now, the last thing I want to do here is to teach my Grandmother to suck eggs (as the old saying goes). You know your business inside out and back to front and I'm sure you know where your clients are and how to go about finding them or you wouldn't be wanting to grow your business. However, at this stage I would recommend spending some time reflecting on the following:

- Where have your clients come from historically?
- What marketing activities have worked best for you?
- What new marketing activities could you consider? For example, asking clients for referrals, increasing social media activity, website optimisation, and new online and offline networking opportunities.

My point here is that once you have found your perfect new team member, you need to be able to follow up on your promise to give them work. You need to manage their expectations of when you will be giving them work, and the expectations of your new clients.

Compliance and legalities

Yes, I know this is a dry topic, but I thought it was important to briefly highlight the issues you need to consider as you start working with associates. Once it's no longer just you in your business there might be any number of legal and compliance issues you need to address, examples of these are:

Insurance

Does your insurance cover the work being done for you by your associates? Do they need their own insurance? What process do you have in place to ensure your associates renew their insurance? I would recommend contacting your insurance provider to ask these questions and to make sure you are adequately protected.

Associate contracts

I talked about putting associate contracts in place in the growing your team section above.

Data Protection

Do you have this written into your associate contracts? GDPR has become such a big issue and it's important for you to set out clearly the responsibilities of you, your associate and your clients.

Professional governing bodies

Are you a member of a professional governing body? Do you need to inform them that you are now using associates? Do your associates also need to become members?

Looking after your team

OK, so you have your team around you. Great! The world is good, and you can now put your feet up and start to reap the rewards. Wrong! This is just the beginning for you and although you are no longer working at the delivery end of your business you still need to consider how you are going to retain your team and build for the future. After all you are only as strong as the team around you, particularly now you have taken a step back from the metaphorical coalface – what would happen if your team member up and left you? How would you cope with the workload? What repercussions would you and your business experience?

You need to make sure your team members are happy, as individuals, as team members, and as part of your business in its entirety. They are your business now. You are still important obviously, but it is your newly recruited team members that are having direct contact with your clients, and they will have the potential to make or break your business. Microbusinesses are by their very nature tiny enterprises and they need to be treated with kid gloves to ensure success and longevity.

Yes, I know this all sounds a little hard hitting and difficult, but you can very easily mitigate the risk and ensure your longevity by changing your role in the business from that of business owner and doer of all tasks, to business owner and leader.

Become a leader

So how do you start going about this I hear you ask? Well, I certainly didn't wake up one morning and suddenly have great leadership skills, and I know for a fact that however hard I work at trying to be a good leader I do sometimes get it wrong. The key here is to relax a little and develop your skills one step at a time.

I am not a leadership guru by any means, but I live my life, including my business life, with the opinion that other people matter. Sounds simple doesn't it? Well it is really. If you consider other people to be just as important, and sometimes more important, as you then you are well on your way to success. There are lots of books that you could read on leadership, and there are numerous courses both online and in person that you could attend, and I encourage you to do both. However, I would like to tell you about the six key things that I think make a good microbusiness leader.

Delegation and empowerment

Ask yourself, are you delegating effectively? It sounds like a great idea to recruit a team member but if you always insist on doing everything yourself what's the point? Since setting up my business I have often told myself that 'it'll be quicker just to do it myself', or 'I'll do a better job, so I'll do it myself', but is that true?

If you take these questions too far and end up doing the work yourself, what is the cost to you? You will run out of time, and you will create stress. In other words, you will have too little time and too much to do. This is not the route to being a Thousandaire! This is the route to overwork and burnout!

If you want someone else to do the work, then you need to give them the freedom to do it without peering over their shoulder at every opportunity making sure they are doing it 'just the way you would'. Delegation is about trust. Without high levels of trust, you won't sleep a wink until you know the work has been done and that your client is happy. I remember the first time I delegated work to a new team member, it was scary, and it was difficult, but I did it anyway.

Firstly, trust in your own decisions. After all you wouldn't have taken on a team member that didn't have the right skills and characteristics, would you?

Secondly, trust in the person doing the work – will they ask you for help if they need it? Are they able to make intelligent decisions based on good information? Will they let you know if they make a mistake?

If you have answered yes to these three questions then delegate the work, empower them to make decisions and move on.

Transparency

Once you have successfully delegated work to your team you have to accept, on the grounds that we are all human beings and not machines, that mistakes will sometimes be made. Nobody is perfect, even you, and mistakes will undoubtedly happen. The important thing is how they are dealt with.

What would you prefer, mistakes to be brushed under the carpet and ignored or lied about, or a phone call from your team member letting you know what has happened and with options to provide a solution? This is the point at which you can discuss the way forward and how to remedy the mistake.

If you nurture a culture of open, honest and transparent communication within your team you will know that any mistakes are dealt with in an open, honest and transparent way.

Responsibility

As a business owner everything that happens within my business is my responsibility. Everything that goes well and conversely everything that goes wrong is my responsibility. Delegation is not about relinquishing that responsibility to others. You want your team members to take ownership of the work they are doing for you, you want them to make decisions on your behalf, and you want them to hold up their hands when things don't go quite to plan, but, as the business owner you are ultimately responsible for it all.

Once you have created a transparent, open and honest communication culture then you need to enhance this by being supportive and approachable. Whatever the problem, it should be all about finding a solution, and not pointing the finger of blame.

Commitment and support

You may no longer be involved with the nitty gritty part of the work, but you are still part of the team, and sometimes you will need to roll up your sleeves and help. This is an absolute in my book. If a client needs work doing, and your team members are burning out trying to hit deadlines, you need to help. You need to help, and you need to support.

Being a leader is sometimes about leading by example. It's about doing what I do rather than doing what I say. After all it is still your business, isn't it? Being committed to your team and providing support as and when required is all part and parcel of being a business owner as well as being a leader.

Positivity

Don't take yourself too seriously. Enjoy your time at work and enjoy your developing relationship with your team members. If you are too uptight and controlling, you won't get the best out of your team. Talk to them about their holidays, arrange team meetings and events. Your positivity will only enhance their experience of working within your business.

Their happiness matters

How you impact on your team members matters. Everything you do as an individual, as a business and as part of the wider team must be based on respecting the self-esteem, feelings and opinions of everyone else.

That is not to say that you can't have a difference of opinion, or on occasion need to give feedback that may not be welcome, but how you communicate with your team members needs to be a conscious and positive experience. Whatever the conversation, always remember, their happiness matters.

They will leave one day – get over it!

A final word to the wise on taking on team members, nurturing them to become a really valued member of the team, delegating work to them so you don't need to do it anymore, and coming to rely on them more and more as time moves on - they will leave one day - get over it!

However lovely they may be, and however well you treat them, they are always going to sit you down one day and tell you the news you have been dreading. They may have another job, they may be retiring, or it might be one of any number of reasons, but the reality is, your wonderful team members are one day going to leave your business. They are not leaving you, don't take it personally, they are leaving the business (at least that should be the case). It is a business decision and you need to treat it as such. Let them go happily and with good grace. It may be tricky for a while filling the gap but with a good team around you, and by going back to the recruitment drawing board you will soon be back to 'business as usual'.

I could talk all day about the benefits of building a good team within your business. They are numerous and a good solid team will enable you to grow your business beyond the time and skills available to just you.

I want to tell you about the time when having a great team really showed its benefits to me in a clear and tangible way. I had five team members at the time, all working very effectively with clients, and all working well as colleagues, sharing work and using each other's expertise and availability to ensure all client work was being handled in the best possible way.

The situation arose that one team member needed to take a few months off work for personal reasons. Now, this could have been a total calamity, it could have created worry and stress about how our client work would be dealt with. What actually happened was that a few conversations took place amongst the team to decide who would take on the responsibility of the workload, we talked to our clients to inform them of the situation and who would be stepping in to make sure they were fully supported, and on the date agreed our client work continued without a hitch.

Our clients received seamless support. The only thing that changed for them was the name of the person providing the service.

My team member could take time off with the knowledge that once she was ready to return to work the client work could easily be transferred back to her. My business continued as normal. The only change was that everyone was a little bit busier than before.

I truly couldn't have done that all by myself.

The Thousandaire model is based upon building a team of associates, changing your focus from business doer to business leader, and enabling you to create a robust and flexible business that feeds into your Thousandaire Sweet Spot.

This chapter has given you the tools to make that happen. Remember though it's not only important to recruit and nurture your team, it's also important to understand the ups and downs that you might come across as you grow. That's what the next chapter is all about, how to keep it going and the challenges you might face.

Key Points

- Keeping your clients happy is your top priority

- Recruiting associates rather than employees is simpler for most microbusinesses

- Finding the right people is absolutely key – have robust recruitment processes and trust your instincts

- Ensure you are legally compliant and have the correct insurance in place

- Manage expectations – be clear with clients and your new associates about workloads

- Become a business leader, not a business doer – empower others in your business to do the work rather than micromanage them

Chapter Eight
KEEPING IT GOING

> "Patience and perseverance have a magical
> effect before which difficulties disappear
> and obstacles vanish."
>
> John Quincy Adams

I know from experience how wonderful business highs are, but how dreadful business lows can make me feel. Over the years I have learnt one critical thing however – the highs and the lows will come; they are both inevitable - that's life!

Business, like life, will sometimes throw you a curveball. What I now try and remember when my curveballs come is that it is not the actual curveball that creates the problem, it is how I react to them that is the problem.

Like life, dealing with the happy times when everything is going well, is easy. We don't even need to try, do we? But, having the self-awareness, strategies and strength to deal with the bad times can me much harder. It's the same in business. It is easy to deal with the good stuff, getting new clients, increasing your turnover, running a successful marketing campaign etc. But it is how we deal with the bad stuff that makes or breaks both us as business owners and our business itself. We need to be resilient. We need what I call 'bouncebackability'.

So how can you achieve this? Well a better question for me would be, 'how did I achieve this'? How did I go from being a nervous wreck whenever things didn't go to plan (and I am not exaggerating here) to someone with bouncebackability?

By the end of the chapter, you'll have a better understanding of:

- some tools to help you 'keep it real' during tough times
- the sort of difficulties that you might encounter while growing your Thousandaire business;
- how amazing you are and how you can get through anything.

Keep it real

Whatever the issue, we all tend to exaggerate the circumstances around our misfortune. We can very quickly escalate something from a simple issue into a huge drama without even trying. Our previous experience, our imagination, our perceptions of what other people may be thinking all contribute to our internal melodrama.

I have learned four specific things over the course of my life in business, all of which help me to balance my internal melodrama with the reality of the situation, and I thought it might be helpful for me to share these with you:

Has anyone died?

My first lesson was from a very dear friend of mine who works as a nurse in an A&E department. Whenever I started talking about the difficulties I was experiencing in my business he would always ask the question 'has anyone died'? Thankfully my answer has always been 'no', but there's nothing like a dose of reality from someone who deals with life and death daily to get things in to perspective. Thank you, John!

I am sure that most of you, like me, don't deal in life and death scenarios in business. I think this makes us lucky. However difficult things can seem sometimes, if you sit back and consider the issue, and I mean really consider how important it is, you will probably come to realise that it doesn't really matter at all. It might matter on a day to day level but on a grand scale it couldn't be less important. Food for thought eh!

Stop it!

My next lesson came when I watched a Bob Newhart clip on YouTube called Stop It! I highly recommend you watching it too. It's a fun and light-hearted approach to overcoming worries and puts everything into perspective. It works on the precept that we don't have to continue with our old way of thinking, we need to just stop it!

The fact and fiction ladder

My third lesson was from Jules Wyman, a confidence coach based in York. I attended a workshop on confidence that Jules was running and out of all the fantastic tools and strategies she shared this is the one that I turn to again and again whenever I need a reality check.

It's called the ladder of fact or fiction and this is what it looks like:

If you are standing on the bottom rung of the ladder, then you are firmly fixed in 'fact'. You are telling yourself the truth about a situation, you are correct in your thinking. The further up the ladder you go the more you start to introduce fiction into your internal story telling. Once you reach the top of the ladder you are making things up entirely, you are telling yourself a story that is just not true.

So, what might you be adding to your story that is firmly in the land of fiction? Here are a few examples of some fiction scenarios that you might include:

- Examples of when things have gone wrong in the past – just because it's happened before doesn't mean it will happen again!
- Embellishment of your story with 'what if' scenarios - Remember your What If Monster?
- Imagining what the results will be – but you don't yet know this, you're just imagining it!

I encourage you to try and stay on the bottom 'fact' rung of your ladder as much as possible. Try asking those closest to you to remind you when you are making things up to fit with your internal story. You might not always like being told, but trust me when I tell you, that you're much better off living in the world of fact than you are in the world of fantasy.

The serenity prayer

Lastly, I rediscovered a favourite prayer by Reinhold Niebuhr. I am not a religious person, but I have always really valued the simplicity of this prayer and reflected on how it is relevant for every problem regardless of the size and complexity:

> God, grant me the serenity to accept
> the things I cannot change,
>
> The courage to change the things I can,
>
> And the wisdom to know the difference.

In other words, if you have a problem, consider what you can do to make a difference. If you can't do anything then move on, the problem may still exist but why waste time worrying about something you can't influence. It also has the opposite effect: if you can do something about the problem, just do it, and you no longer have a problem so move on. You can either do something or you can't. Either way stop worrying. Thought provoking stuff isn't it?

I have in the past spent so much time worrying about how my actions and decisions impact on other people that it sometimes prevented me from taking action. I am happy to say that this has changed. I am still considerate about how my actions impact on other people, but I believe that if my actions and words are delivered with honestly, transparency, respect and kindness then I can't go far wrong. It is always better to deal with things head on than by zig zagging around the issue and dragging it out for everyone involved.

My message here is that things will go wrong for all of us from time to time. Sometimes we start the day feeling as though everything is wonderful and end it feeling like the weight of the world is on our shoulders. This happens to everyone, I'm not special and neither are you when it comes to curveballs swiping in from the side lines. But whatever happens it is rarely as bad as we can think it is. Changing the way in which you respond to your curveballs is what it's all about.

Here are just a few examples of the sort of thing you might have to deal with:

You're going to lose a client

Do you remember how you felt when you got your first client? I most certainly do - I was ecstatic! I was totally ecstatic! It was the starting blocks for me as a self-employed business person. My first client even owned their own helicopter – I was in awe!

Now think about how you felt when you first lost a client? Whatever the reason for losing that client, how did you feel? What did it mean to you? What did it mean to your business?

No clients are going to stay forever. A little like what I said in the previous chapter about your team members leaving you, your clients will leave one day too. They may need to employ someone to do the work you are currently doing for them; they may go out of business; maybe the economy dictates their decision to leave. Whatever their reasons you need to ensure that they never leave because of what you do.

With the number of self-employed people on the rise, and your clients being able to choose who they work with from a growing number of service providers or producers, you need to make sure that they are happy. You need to make sure that the service they want is the service they get. It's all about your customer service being at the very heart of everything you do.

Always remember that it is easier to keep a client than it is to find a new one.

I encourage you at this stage to consider your values and to spend some time reflecting on the following questions:

- What do you do when a client is dissatisfied? What is your process for dealing with this?
- What do you do when things go wrong? Do you hold your hands up and sort it out, or do you 'do an ostrich' and hide your head in the sand and hope it all goes away?
- How do you communicate with your clients? Is it to suit you or to suit what each individual client wants from you?
- When was the last time you asked your clients how happy they are with your service or product?

However hard you try though, sometimes mistakes will be made – we're only human! An example of this was where one of our clients felt that for a very short space of time, she got a 'good secretarial service' instead of the 'Executive PA service' we had promised her.

So, what did we do about this? Well, firstly we read the signs, we listened to our client, we identified the problem and we swiftly resolved it. We had an open and honest conversation with our client during a very short transition period and we gave her that little bit more tender loving care while we fixed the problem. At the end of it we now have a very happy client who is 'delighted with the quality and responsiveness of our support'. Result!

I'm sure that, like me, you won't get it right all the time, but reflecting on these questions and developing a clear plan for how you'll respond will stand you in good stead for when the worst happens.

You're going to have staff issues

However hard you try to find the right team members with the right values and who are the right fit for your business and for your clients, you will still have to deal with staff issues from time to time. These might include under-performance of a team member; a client complaint; lack of commitment; and a bad attitude to you, other team members and worst of all to the client themselves.

Always remember, as I talked about in Chapter Eight, that the happiness of your team members matters. It's so important that they are happy in their work and happy as part of your team. But they still need to provide the level of service that you promise to your clients, and they still need to be committed to you, your business and the rest of the team. They're not doing you a favour, they're contracted to you to do a job, and as such they need to be accountable for the work they do.

In my experience it's always better to have an open and honest conversation as soon as a problem arises. There's really no point in dragging it out for anyone.

Remember, just because you're no longer working on the front line, you're still responsible for the work that is being produced on behalf of your clients. The buck stops with you, so if you don't deal with an issue then it could ultimately reflect on you and your business.

I encourage you to always talk to your team member in an honest and open way about what the problem is. Remember to talk to them about specifics though. The problem is not with them as a person or as a team member, it's about a specific incident or behaviour that needs to be addressed.

It can be a difficult thing to give negative feedback, and I thought it would be helpful for me to share a tool that I have recently discovered that will help you to frame the conversation in a positive way:

The DESC feedback model

This model helps you to effectively describe the behaviour or incident and how it has impacted on you or others in a specific and positive way as follows:

D – Describe

Describe what happened. Take them back to the moment when the incident happened. For example, "do you remember on Tuesday when we were all in team meeting and you refused to make the tea"? Starting with the moment will allow them to recognise and remember the time you are talking about.

E – Express

Express how this behaviour made you feel. For example, "this made me feel very frustrated…". The person you are talking to can't argue with how you are feeling. They are your feelings and you are legitimately allowed to have them.

S – Specifics

Be specific, for example, "because we all take it in turns to make the tea and it was your turn to do this, and at the previous meeting you had promised to make the tea for everyone".

C – Consequences

Let them know what the consequences are. For example, "how do you think this will make the rest of the team feel if you don't contribute as much as they do"?

You're going to want to let a nightmare client go

Wow! This is a very tough thing to do!

I once started work with a new client and I was excited and raring to go. As his PA I was expected to manage his diary and international travel itinerary. I was asked to organise a very complex meeting schedule in Sweden. Now remember, this was my first day working with this client, I had no idea who the people were that I was arranging for him to meet, I had no idea if he had met them before, whether they were good friends, family or business contacts etc. In fact, I was totally in the dark. I had been given no remit on how long the meetings should be, whether he enjoyed meeting over lunch or dinner etc.

So, what did I do? Well I asked him if he could provide me with a few pointers. Not unreasonable at all I thought. His response? "You're the PA, sort it!"

This client lasted one day! It certainly wasn't an ideal scenario for me or for him, but I could see that our values were not aligned, I could see that if we continued working together it would result in stress for both of us, and I had the self-awareness to know that this relationship was never going to work. I'm proud that I stopped working with him, I'm proud that I had the strength to see past the financial impact and focus on what was right for me at the time.

There's no beating about the bush on this, making the decision to let a client go will result in reduced income. It's a fact. But… think back to Chapter One where you considered your Thousandaire Sweet Spot and your vision, remember why you set up your business in the first place, and ask yourself:

- Does this client contribute to my happiness?
- Is this client the sort of person I imagined myself working with when I developed my vision?
- Would I want one of my team members to put up with this sort of nonsense?
- What are my non-negotiables? What will I put up with and what won't I put up with? Remember you're a professional service provider now and not an employee!

Remember, you have a choice on behalf of your business, you have a choice on behalf of yourself, and perhaps most importantly once you've built your Thousandaire business, you have a choice on behalf of your team members – do you want them to work with someone who treats them badly, who disrespects their boundaries, who has unreasonable expectations and who is quite simply a nightmare to work with? I'm pretty sure that your answer will be an outstanding NO!

I implore you, don't work with people who don't respect you and what you do, or your business. I promise you, there are plenty of other clients out there who will.

You might lose a team member and a client at the same time

This has happened to me once and it was the most upsetting thing that has happened to me since setting up my business. In simple terms, my team member started working directly with my client, cutting me out of the equation, and leaving me with one less client and a huge problem sorting out the other client work that still needed to be resourced. It was a nightmare!

Now, having got this far in the book you'll know by now that everything I do in my business is driven by my values. I trust people, and when that trust is broken it feels personal and it really hurts. It was an extremely stressful time, it took up all my energy, I lost sleep, I spent hours on the phone to my solicitor, and I almost gave up on my business.

Hopefully you'll never have to deal with this but if you do then I suggest you consider the following:

Contracts

As I talked about in Chapter Seven, make sure your contracts clearly lay out the rules on non-solicitation of clients. Your contract solicitor will be able to advise you on this.

Interview

Have a frank and straightforward conversation on the non-solicitation of clients during the interview for your team members. Make it clear that your clients are your clients and not theirs. I now unapologetically do the following:

- Ask them what would they do if a client approached them with an offer to work direct? How would they react? What would their response be? Could they imagine a scenario when this might be tempting to them? How do their own personal values align with doing something like this?

- I also make it totally clear that the solicitation of clients will not be tolerated, and that further action will be taken.

I'm hopeful that you won't ever have to deal with this scenario but if you do please remember one thing: you can't control what other people do. You can only control what you do and how you react to what other people do. Try to remain calm and ask yourself 'has anyone died'?

You're going to have money wobbles

It's a fact for all of us that at some point you're probably going to have some money wobbles. You're going to have moments when it just feels too financially hard to keep going and you might be tempted to throw your hands in the air and give in to the struggle. So, what sort of money wobbles might you encounter? These are the three wobbles that I come across from time to time and I hope that by sharing my experiences here it will help you:

You'll have a cash flow crisis

There are two pitfalls that you might fall into when it comes to having a cash flow crisis.

Firstly, it might feel like a good idea to work directly with your clients again. I know very well how tempting it can be to not have to pay your team members for work if you do it yourself. This may give you a short term gain financially but remember your vision and don't give in to what seems like a good opportunity to earn money now. The long-term impact of this is that you are back where you started. Doing all the work and being restricted by the number of hours in the day, weeks in the month and months in the year etc.

Secondly, you might consider delaying payment to your suppliers and team members. I will be honest with you here, I have really struggled at times to pay myself anything at all. But I believe in running an ethical business that pays suppliers before I pay myself. Perhaps this makes me a fool and perhaps I am not a business genius, and this may be why I will never reach millionaire status, but I do believe in paying my bills on time.

My suppliers are also microbusinesses trying to make ends meet, and as their client I am responsible for paying for the service they provide. Apart from the fact that your team members will soon leave you if you don't pay them on time, you should want to pay them on time. You should value and appreciate what it is they are doing for you.

Like I said in Chapter Seven about building your team and leadership skills, their happiness matters! Your suppliers are not just a skills resource for your business, they are also human beings trying to make a living and be happy. It is your responsibility to pay them on time and it is your responsibility to respect them as individuals and as business owners.

I know that many businesses thrive on delaying payments to suppliers, and seem to think that this is appropriate, but I disagree. Treat others as you wish to be treated yourself. Be ethical.

Clients will ask for a discount

Many years ago, in a former life, I worked in Egypt, where I learned a lesson that is still very valuable to me in business.

Every time a product or service was bought, it was traditional to haggle over the price. The best advice I received on haggling was to always ensure you paid a price you were happy with – whatever that figure was.

In other words, it's more important to feel you're getting value for money, whatever price you pay in the end. Your clients have chosen you to deliver to them the service or product you are selling. It is not always about price, but it is always about value for money.

My best practice is not to negotiate on price. I find it makes much more sense to add as much value as I can, where I can, and always look for creative ways to benefit my clients.

As Virtual Assistants, this involves the same kind of attention to detail as a good full-time Personal Assistant – we pre-empt our clients' needs, share their business goals and make completely sure we are way ahead on all the work we're doing for them.

Good clients naturally receive more value the longer they work with us, or any other freelance business-to-business service provider, as you build up a good working relationship over time.

You naturally become more familiar with their working styles and priorities, their business and its clients – which means you can add tons of invaluable background knowledge and efficiency to everything you do for them.

It's a better alternative to being in the position where your charges are so low, you've inadvertently put yourself under pressure to cut corners in your work, just so that you can make ends meet.

Low prices don't automatically mean you're giving value for money – quality workmanship is more beneficial to you and your clients.

You'll forget to value yourself

Know your worth as a leader, as a business development person, and as the person taking the risks. I have always struggled with charging my clients one price but paying my team a lower rate. I struggle with this because I like to think that I am a fair and reasonable person. But that said, my clients come because of my hard work and commitment to the business, my marketing activities, my investment in websites and other marketing material etc. There must be a value placed in this work.

I would like to invite you at this point to take a few moments to reflect on what your value is in your business. What do you do that nobody else can do? What is unique about you? What is your role now that you have a team around you?

Is the price right?

Whether you encounter financial curveballs or not, chances are you'll need to review your pricing as you become a Thousandaire. It's important as you grow your Thousandaire business to make sure that what you are charging your clients and customers covers your costs and pays you enough money to thrive (Remember your Thousandaire Sweet Spot).

Consider what you are currently charging. Have you researched the market rate of what you offer? What do your competitors charge? Where do you currently sit on the pricing scale? Are you cheap or expensive or somewhere in between? Have you reviewed your prices since you started?

It's easy when you first start out to think that you need to keep your prices low to encourage business, but the negative impact of this can be three-fold:

1. You might be keeping the market value of your product or service low for yourself and for everybody else.
2. It's always hard to increase your price in the future. It's much easier to go in high from the start and sell your service based on added value and unique selling points.
3. When you start building your team you won't be able to pay them. Simple. Unless your prices are high enough you won't have any flexibility around paying for the team that are going to help your business to grow.

Ok, that's enough doom and gloom! Reflecting on what might go wrong may seem a little counter-intuitive, it might feel a bit depressing, but it's not. It's about preparing for the worst-case scenario and developing a contingency plan. Better to think about it now while you're all fired up about the future than to have to think about it when it happens and being totally unprepared.

I want you to love your Thousandaire business and part of that is remembering all the great stuff that you can draw upon to support you during your difficult times.

Use your business buddies

I talked in Chapter Two about building a support network around you. Being a microbusiness owner can be a very lonely existence, particularly if you work from home, and having business friends that you can call upon in times of need is essential.

When times are tough use your network. Who can you confide in? Who can you turn to for help and advice? Who are your business allies? There are plenty of online networks available via social media, and in my mind it's always a good idea to have 'real life' networks too – see what networking events are happening in your local area.

Believe in yourself – you're amazing!

If you don't believe in you, then why would anyone else?

This may sound harsh but it's true. Self-belief comes from within you, the hint is in the word 'self'. Those around you can help to nurture your self-belief, but ultimately it needs to come from you.

I know that without self-belief I would never have set up in business in the first place. That said, there are times when things happen in both my personal and my business life that make me wobble, some very significant and life changing. My self-belief is fragile, and I need to nurture it, look after it, and help it to thrive.

We need to be kind to ourselves and not beat ourselves up when things don't go to plan. Remember, these curveballs don't pick us because we're special, we're not! They affect every one of us at some time.

Have faith in your own abilities

When things go wrong focus on times when things have gone well. Try to remember the times when you have succeeded, when you have been proud of yourself, when you have made the right decision.

I often make a note of things that go well. Sometimes these are only tiny things like how I felt when I finished a tricky piece of work; or when a difficult conversation went better than I could have ever imagined. Sometimes, it's the big things, like taking on a fabulous new team member, or achieving something extraordinary on behalf of a client. It can be whatever you want it to be but writing these things down will give you time to reflect on your successes and it will provide you with a solid base to return to when the wobbles come along.

Consider the implications of not doing something

When I come across anything that feels scary, like dealing with a difficult client or talking to a team member about a client complaint, I try to consider the implications of not doing it. How will I feel if I don't do something? What will the result of that be? How will it impact on my business right now and in the future?

In contrast, how will I feel once the issue has been dealt with?

It's often not nearly as scary as we think it will be. I always look back on these scary moments and wonder what I was worried about. We are all very good at imagining how bad things can be but not so good at trying to make our imagination think about how brilliant things can be. Think back to the fact and fiction ladder I talked about earlier in this chapter – where are you on that ladder?

My mother taught me a great lesson in life – the only people who don't make mistakes are the people who don't do anything (I think she got that from Albert Einstein). I, like my mother, also have a few wise words for you – don't beat yourself up, after all you are only human.

Business hiccups will come and go, but like life things get better eventually. Some problems you will have dealt with well and others less well, but right or wrong, good or bad, you need to move on and learn from your experience. Having a learning mindset will always stand you in good stead. Expecting yourself to make mistakes, expecting your team to make mistakes, but being forgiving and ultimately learning from our mistakes is crucial. It's all a powerful learning curve. I certainly wouldn't be writing this book today if I had never made mistakes – and boy there were some whoppers!

Values are so important when you're dealing with anything tricky, whether it's a customer complaint or perhaps you've just made a huge mistake which makes you want to throw up (trust me I've been there!). If you can use your values as a backstop, consider the reality check lessons I talked about earlier in this chapter, remember to be a sunflower, and draw on your inner strengths, then, in my opinion, you can't go far wrong.

Key Points

- It's not about what goes wrong (because sooner or later, something will), it's about how you react to it

- Keep yourself grounded. What feels like a catastrophe is probably not that big a deal in the grand scheme of things (to quote my friend John: "Who died?")

- Most client and associate curveballs can be dealt with through open and honest communication – face things head on.

- Financial curveballs are difficult but stick to your values and stay ethical.

- Don't forget to value yourself – both financially and emotionally!

CONCLUSION

THE END OF THE BEGINNING...

> 'Now this is not the end. It is not even the beginning of the end. But it is, perhaps, the end of the beginning.'
> Winston Churchill

Oh, my goodness! What an amazing journey this has been! I hope you're proud of what you have achieved, and how far along the road you are to transforming your vision into your reality. I hope that I've given you all the tools and encouragement you need to go even further. Your Thousandaire Sweet Spot is well within your reach now and all you need to do is 'go get it'!

Throughout this book I've guided you through the process of your business growth in easy to follow step-by-step stages. You've learned about vision and goal setting, the importance of knowing what success looks like for you, how to align your values with your behaviours, the ups and downs of recruiting your team members, strategies to successfully working from home and tips on how to improve your inner strength and confidence. The list goes on…

But what does it all mean? What does my life look like now?

Well, I'm still very much involved in my business. It is my baby after all and that hasn't changed. But my focus has changed. I love my business. I love my team. I love my clients. I also love the fact that I can now focus on things other than the day to day service that my business is paid for, like the recruitment of new team members, personal development, and nurturing team and client relationships – after all without them my business wouldn't exist. They matter more to me than anything!

I can also be found walking my dog, Ziggy, along the River Foss most days, and sometimes Ziggy and I take long walks along the coast or on the North Yorkshire Moors. I used to think of this time as unproductive, but I've changed my mind about that. I use my dog walking time to think and reflect on my business. If I have a difficult decision to make, or if I've got a dilemma I need to think through, I do this on my dog walks. The exercise, solitude and fresh air help me to think. In fact, most decisions I make for my business are made during one of our walks.

In 2018 I took my walking to the next level, and I raised over £10,000 for two charities supporting vulnerable children by hiking and wild camping the 109-mile route of The Cleveland Way over 7 consecutive days. I wouldn't have been able to do that without my Thousandaire business - I just wouldn't have had the time, energy or head-space to manage the fundraising and all the training to get me fit enough. Can you even imagine the amount of thinking I did on that walk?

I'm also spending a lot of time focusing on my leadership development and growth. For the most part since I set up my business in 2008, I've pretty much made stuff up as I've gone along. Yes, it has all worked out fine, but I know that with a little more strategic thinking and a little more knowledge I would have had a far easier time of it. This is my time to learn and grow as a leader so that the next stage of my business growth is easier than the first – I could do with a book like this actually!

As you take your next steps towards realising your Thousandaire Sweet Spot here are a few extra nuggets of advice that I hope will help you along the way:

Baby Steps

> 'Sometimes the smallest step in the right direction ends up being the biggest step of your life. Tiptoe if you must but take a step.'
> Naeem Callaway

Whatever your business, and whatever your aspirations, achieving your goals is not going to happen overnight. If you do something every day to move forwards you will eventually get where you want to go. However hard it might feel sometimes keep reminding yourself that every step forward is now a step behind you. However small each step might be, every one of them is propelling you forward towards your goal.

Teams rock!

> 'We are not a team because we work together. We are a team because we respect, trust and care for each other.'
> Vala Afshar

Remember that you can't do it alone. The people who walk alongside you, who support your business through good and bad times, your team members, your business allies, and your family and friends. Respect and value what they do for you.

These are the people who made this happen for you. These people are part of your success. You're a team and you rock!

Remember your big picture

> 'Never tell me the sky's the limit when
> there are footprints on the moon'
> Unknown

Remember your Thousandaire Sweet Spot. Remember what success looks like for you. Whatever happens keep focussed on what you are trying to achieve. Keep your vision board close to you and use it to inspire and motivate you. You can change it if you want to, it's your vision and you can do whatever you want with it. Just don't let anyone else change it for you!

Be a sunflower

> 'Keep your face to the sunshine and you cannot see
> the shadows. It's what the sunflowers do.'
> Helen Keller

Do you remember the sunflower I talked about in Chapter One? I explained that a sunflower will move throughout the day to face the sun, is flexible enough to bend with the wind, and yet remains firmly rooted. Whatever happens to it, whatever is going on around it, it is always a sunflower. So, move toward what nourishes you and be flexible with what you expect from other people yet remain firmly rooted in your values and your vision. A sunflower is resilient. Be a sunflower.

What next?

It's been an absolute pleasure writing this book. It hasn't been easy, or quick, but it has certainly fulfilled and challenged me. I have massively enjoyed the process, and I'm proud to be able to share my journey with you, and excited about the collaboration and community we can build together. Between us we can forge connections while we learn how to strengthen and grow our businesses so that we can survive any curveballs life throws our way. We can help ourselves and others to realise our microbusiness dreams. How fab is that!

You're already part of an amazing Thousandaire community that is growing and thriving through this book. You've heard all about my journey, and now I would love to hear about and help you on your journey, so if you would like to continue learning and growing alongside our online community please join in at:

Facebook page – **Catherine Adamson - Author Mentor Speaker**

The Thousandaire website and blog – **www.catherineadamson.co.uk**

I look forward to seeing you there, it's all totally free and you will receive a very warm welcome.

Thank you for sharing my journey with me. I hope it's made a difference. All that's left to say is good luck and let me know how you get on. Now – take out your Thousandaire journal and start planning!

Appendices

Sample person specification 203

Sample job description 205

Expenditure chart 207

Sample person specification

Skills, Knowledge and Experience

- Significant experience of providing support at Board level (minimum 5 years)
- Significant experience of managing multiple high-level diaries
- Commercially aware
- Able to create written material with flair
- Excellent verbal skills i.e. face to face, telephone and video conferencing
- Numeracy skills
- Able to organise, plan and prioritise tasks
- Experience of booking national and international travel and accommodation
- Proficient in using Microsoft or Apple software
- Excellent typing and transcription skills
- 5 GCSE's or equivalent

Characteristics

- Passionate about customer service
- Common sense approach and good judgement
- Calm approach to changing priorities
- High levels of integrity
- Good interpersonal skills
- Communicates clearly and competently
- Able to listen actively
- Dependable
- Accountable
- Able to work without supervision and capable of using own initiative

- Flexible and motivated team member
- Approachable and cooperative
- Tenacious and resilient
- Quick and enthusiastic learner
- Drive to achieve results
- Willingness to learn and develop new skills

General

- Desire for Kaleidoscope to be successful
- Has own office facilities – printer & scanner, professional space, computer & software, business phone line, transcription tools
- Available for work Monday to Friday on a flexible and part-time basis

Sample job description

Job Title:	Executive Virtual Assistant (Self Employed)
Responsible To:	The Executive Virtual Assistant is responsible to the Executive Team Leader who in turn is responsible to the business owner
Hours of Work:	Part-time / flexible hours to cover over five days (Monday-Friday)

Purpose of the Job

To provide professional Executive Virtual Assistant support to Executive Coaches, Non-Executive Directors and other high-level clients, and to respond in a timely fashion to all client requirements.

To actively add value to the service provided by Kaleidoscope and to continually work toward the development and growth of all client and team relationships.

To contribute to the successful operation of Kaleidoscope and the achievement of objectives set by the business owner.

Responsibilities

The duties below are not for every client and are not exclusive. You will need to be flexible enough to respond to a variety of client requirements, with the support of the Kaleidoscope team, which may include the following:

Diary and Email Management
- Managing multiple high-level diaries.

- Communicating with client contacts by phone and email.
- Monitoring, actioning and updating work in progress.
- Organising travel and accommodation as per the client requirements.
- Managing multiple client and internal email accounts.

Communications
- Close collaboration with clients to ensure they are fully supported.
- Attendance at regular virtual team meetings and regular 1:1 calls with the business owner.

Typing
- Audio transcription of minutes, reports and emails as required.

Research
- Conduct research, compile data, and prepare papers for presentation to the client.

Other
- Ensuring all Kaleidoscope internal processes are adhered to.
- To be an active, integral and supportive member of the Kaleidoscope team.
- To act as an ambassador for Kaleidoscope, ensuring your behaviours reflect the values of the business.

Expenditure chart

Expenditure chart	MONTH 1	MONTH 2	MONTH 3
Mortgage/Rent			
Council Tax			
Water Rates			
Gas & Electricity			
Home Telephone, TV, Broadband etc			
TV Licence			
Home Insurance			
Car Insurance			
Pet Insurance			
Car Service & MOT			
Road Tax			
Petrol			
Mobile Phone			
TV Subscriptions e.g. Netflix			
Magazine Subs.			
Gym Membership			
Groceries			
Savings			
Holidays			
TOTAL EXPENDITURE			
TOTAL INCOME			
THE GAP (how much you have left, or how much more you need to earn)			

Catherine Adamson

Author | Mentor | Speaker

www.ingramcontent.com/pod-product-compliance
Lightning Source LLC
Chambersburg PA
CBHW042137160426
43200CB00020B/2966